Bernice Sandler

and the

Fight for Title IX

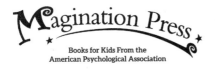

**Books for Kids From the
American Psychological Association**

Copyright © 2022 by Jen Barton. Introduction copyright © 2022 by Margaret Dunkle. Endmatter text "How to Be an Activist" copyright © 2022 by Sage Carson. Illustrations copyright © 2022 by Sarah Green. Published in 2022 by Magination Press, an imprint of the American Psychological Association. All rights reserved. Except as permitted under the United States Copyright Act of 1976, no part of this publication may be reproduced or distributed in any form or by any means, or stored in a database or retrieval system, without the prior written permission of the publisher.

Magination Press is a registered trademark of the American Psychological Association. Order books at maginationpress.org or call 1-800-374-2721.

Book design by Rachel Ross
Cover printed by Phoenix Color, Hagerstown, MD
Interior printed by Sheridan Books, Inc., Chelsea, MI

Cataloging-in-Publication Data is on file at the Library of Congress.
ISBN: 978-1-4338-3946-7

Manufactured in the United States of America
10 9 8 7 6 5 4 3 2 1

Bernice Sandler

and the

Fight for Title IX

by **Jen Barton**

illustrated by **Sarah Green**

Magination Press · Washington, DC
American Psychological Association

Table of Contents

This book is dedicated to the first woman president of the United States, whoever she may be. Though Bunny Sandler didn't live to see a woman hold the highest office of the land, her tireless efforts for women's equality helped pave the way.

Like Bunny said,
"The first woman president is out there. We just don't know who she is yet." Someday we will—*JB*

Dedicated to all the activists who paved the path for me, and all the ones to come—*SG*

The Accidental Activist Who Became the Godmother of Title IX

by Margaret Dunkle

We've all had a hero—someone we looked up to and saw as larger than life. Think for a minute. Who is that person for you? Who has that strength of character, nobility of purpose, vision for a fairer, better world, and the gumption and smarts to get there?

For me, that person was Dr. Bernice Sandler, known to all by her childhood name, "Bunny." In the summer of 1972, I was fortunate enough to join her new Project on Women at the Association of American Colleges. I had just turned 25. Title IX—the landmark law promising equal education to women and girls—had just been signed into law.

In some ways, Bunny was an accidental activist. She didn't start out to raise a ruckus. Then her university slammed the door to academic jobs in her face, simply because she was a woman. Rather than complain of a broken nose (or bruised pride), she dug in and figured out how to pry open that very door.

She threw everything she had into righting that wrong—not only for herself, but for other professors, and students, too. And she had a lot to throw: boundless energy... stick-to-itiveness and tenacity that wore out opponents and inspired those by her side... a gift for words and speech... a nerdy ability to sniff out important information hidden in plain sight (such as a footnote no one else bothered to read)... an uncanny knack to be the first to spot the next issue to tackle (from sports to the chilly classroom climate to sexual assault)... disarming charm, ready wit, and an infectious laugh... a generosity of spirit that brought out the best in those around her... and, last but not least, brains and savvy.

The fight for Title IX was indeed worth waging. You probably don't realize what a difference Title IX has made, compared to when your mom or grandmother were kids. Before Title IX, a university could put your application—whether to become an undergrad freshman or for law school or medical school—at the bottom of the pile just because you were a girl. Your school sports opportunities would be either none or few and under-funded. There were no rules to prevent sexual harassment or being creepily touched by a teacher or another student. You could be expelled for being pregnant, while your boyfriend graduated and captained the football team. And so much more, from scholarships to classes, clubs to counseling....

While fighting for fair policies, Bunny also made everyone around her a better version of themselves. She assigned me—whose athletic prowess peaked at age eight, playing badminton on our front lawn

Margaret Dunkle, age 8, playing badminton in her front yard.

with my Dad—to figure out what Title IX meant for sports. She somehow convinced everyone, including me, that I—the youngest person in the room—should be the first chair of the National Coalition for Women and Girls in Education, even as Title IX's very survival was on the line. She then mentored and supported me to prove herself right.

Bunny Sandler taught me that I could do more...be more...make more of a difference...than I ever dreamed. The message of this book is that you can, too.

Margaret Dunkle, left, and Bunny, right, Fall 1977. At the time, Margaret was the Associate Director, and Bunny the Director, of the Project on the Status & Education of Women for the Association of American Colleges.

Chapter 1

Too Strong for a Woman

"Thank you, Bernice Sandler!! You gave me my chance at a great life and your impact will forever be felt by many. Forever grateful. Title IX wouldn't have happened without you."
—*Abby Wambach, Olympic Gold Medalist*

In the spring of 1969 Bernice "Bunny" Sandler graduated from the University of Maryland with a doctorate degree in Counseling and Personnel Services. She was 41 years old. She had teaching experience, excellent credentials, and faith in a system that was about to completely let her down.

In addition to being a wife and a mother during graduate school, Bunny held a part-time job teaching at the university. She hoped her experience and new degree would help her get a full-time spot. As luck would have it, seven positions were available. Despite being extremely qualified—she had after all just graduated with a doctorate from the very school she was applying to—she wasn't getting any traction.

She couldn't figure it out, so she asked a colleague what he thought. Why wasn't she being considered?

"Face it," her friend said. "You come on too strong for a woman."

Though Bunny couldn't have known it, the world shifted in that moment. For that casually discriminatory comment would not only change her life, taking it in new and exciting directions, but it also planted the seeds of Title IX, a law that would soon prohibit sex discrimination in any educational institution that received federal funds. With just 37 key words, this new law would arguably become the most important legislation for the equality of women and girls since suffragists won the right for women to vote in 1920.

But back then, Bunny wasn't inspired. She wasn't a feminist. She wasn't even mad. "I went home that night and I cried," she remembered. Bunny blamed herself for speaking up in staff meetings, and even for participating in class as a graduate student. She thought it was her fault. She believed what her colleague had said. She thought she really was "too strong for a woman."

It was her husband, Jerrold Sandler, who suggested she'd been a victim of sex discrimination. "Are there strong men in the department?" he asked. "If so, it's not you." Bunny quickly realized he was right. Still, she wasn't sure about the label. The term "sexism" wasn't commonly used or understood back then, and "sex discrimination" sounded like something "those feminists" said. And Bunny wasn't comfortable being part of the women's movement yet. The press described feminists as "abrasive," "unfeminine," and "man-hating."

"Surely," she thought, "I was not like that."

But as Bunny continued her job search, trying to find work near her home in Silver Spring, Maryland, she began to see a pattern. In one interview, a researcher spent nearly an hour explaining he didn't hire women because when their kids got sick, they missed work. Though sexist and inappropriate at any time, Bunny wasn't even a young mother. Her two daughters, Deborah and Emily, were in high school. But it didn't seem to matter. Later, a counselor at an employment agency reviewed her resume and remarked she wasn't really a professional, but instead just a housewife who had gone back to school.

Comments like these, and this kind of thinking, were common at the time. Women were expected to be wives and mothers, and not much more. Many universities, including some Ivy league schools like Harvard and Columbia, didn't admit women, and wouldn't for years to come. Women couldn't serve on a jury in all 50 states until 1973. And until 1974, banks could refuse to issue credit cards to unmarried women or require a married woman's husband to sign for the card. Women trying to buy property or secure a home loan faced similar restrictions. Sex discrimination was everywhere.

Bunny realized the discrimination she'd experienced since graduation was just the tip of the iceberg. She began re-thinking other situations. Like when she'd applied for financial aid during graduate school and a man on the phone explained they didn't give many scholarships to women, especially married women. Even less, he continued, to married women with children. Back then, many people thought money used on a woman's education was wasted, that women only went to college to get their "Mrs. degree" (a derogatory way of saying women went to college just to find a husband!). And women with children were considered an especially bad risk, since their primary responsibilities were already at home. Women couldn't be allowed to take up precious educational resources a man might need to support his family, the thinking was, so men were given higher priority for funding.

How many times, Bunny wondered, had this happened over the years? She hadn't been overlooked for the teaching position because she spoke her mind or had opinions. She'd been overlooked because she was a *woman* who spoke her mind and had opinions. It wasn't her fault at all. Bunny started to see things in a whole new light, which meant she couldn't rationalize or dismiss what had happened to her any longer. She began thinking about the growing women's movement. Before long, she saw it in a new way, a way she connected with. Like her mother Ivy, Bunny was a determined problem-solver. And an academic. "When things go wrong in my life," she said, "I start to read about the problem." Bunny put her head down and got to work.

Because sex discrimination was immoral and wrong, Bunny figured it would be illegal, too. She soon discovered it was not—at least not for women and girls in education. Though laws like the Equal Pay Act of 1963 and the Civil Rights Act of 1964 prohibited many forms of discrimination, exemptions existed in laws protecting employees of educational institutions. On top of that, there were no federal laws at all to protect women students from sex discrimination in schools or colleges. These legal holes left many women administrators, professors, and faculty—and all women students—unprotected. Bunny was incredulous. "That doesn't seem fair at all," she thought.

But she wasn't about to quit. Bunny knew Black people had battled discrimination, so she started investigating how civil rights activists ended segregation and fought racial discrimination in schools and colleges. She hoped to find a path, or a clue, to ending sex discrimination in education as well. After months of reading and research, she came to a report written by the U.S. Commission on Civil Rights. In it, she found Presidential Executive Order 11246. President Lyndon Johnson issued this widely unknown Executive Order on September 24, 1965. It prohibited federal contractors from discriminating in employment on the basis of race, color, religion, and national origin. Sex wasn't mentioned. But there was a footnote. And being an academic, Bunny never skipped a footnote.

A WORD ABOUT SEX VS. GENDER page 7

To her surprise and delight, she found exactly what she'd been searching for. On October 13, 1967, President Johnson had amended the Executive Order to include a person's sex! Federal contractors were not only prohibited from discriminating on the basis of race, color, religion, or national origin, but also on the basis of sex.

Sitting at the kitchen table with books and papers spread before her, Bunny nearly fell out of her chair. She knew that the many colleges and universities, like her own University of Maryland, and the most prestigious, like the Ivy Leagues, had major federal contracts. "I actually shrieked aloud," she remembered. Through hard work and determination, Bunny Sandler had found a path to ending sex discrimination in education—at least for employees. Students were a different matter. Indeed, the real battle had just begun.

A Word About Sex vs. Gender

When Bunny was fighting for Title IX and women's equity in education, the terms *sex* and *gender* were used interchangeably by many people. It wasn't until recently that mainstream society began making a distinction between the two. Because of this, the historical contexts used in this book will often discuss "sex" discrimination or equity where today we might use "gender," and sometimes vice versa.

Now we use sex to refer to the anatomical physical characteristics a person is born with. It describes the biological differences between males and females, or what "parts" you have. In the past, sex has been seen as binary—either male or female. Increasingly, there's awareness of people born with a mix of genitalia. This is sometimes called intersex, instead of male or female. About 1 in every 1500 births is intersex.

Gender, on the other hand, speaks more to how you see yourself in society and how society sees you. What does it mean to be a man or a woman? What does it mean to be in between? What are the expectations for behavior, clothes, social interactions, or speech? How do you want to express your femininity and masculinity? The answers to those questions will affect how you present yourself to the world. Importantly, a person's gender expression may not match their biological sex characteristics.

Many people don't feel represented by the definition established for male and female genders and are redefining roles, allowing for a continuum instead of a binary. Moving on that continuum is called gender fluidity.

TRY THIS:

Investigate History

Think of a person, an issue, or an organization that's especially meaningful to you. Maybe it's your church or religion, a relative, your favorite actor, musician, or sports hero. Or maybe your topic is climate change. Chances are, other people have cared about or worked on your subject in the past. Social movements, and family histories too, build on the work and effort of many people over time. Learning the stories of those who came before you can help paint a richer picture and be fulfilling as well as informative.

Spend some time investigating the history and background of your subject. You might go to the library, search online, or conduct interviews if possible. If your subject is large, it may feel overwhelming at first, but pick one area of your subject and start there. Once you've decided on something, learn as much as you can about the essentials of that area: who, what, when, where, why, and how. If you're still interested when you've finished, pick another area and do the same. Before you know it, you'll have a ton of background information on your subject. You might even be able to work your research into a school assignment.

Investigating history lets us learn who and what came before, giving us important context. Bunny's understanding of how civil rights activists had battled for equality and desegregation served as a model for her fight. And when she found the all-important footnote hidden in that congressional report, she knew it wasn't there by chance or luck. Someone had worked to make it happen. She quickly learned about Esther Peterson and how she'd lobbied for "sex" to be included in the footnote as a protected group. Because Esther Peterson had worked hard, Bunny had what she needed. Esther Peterson not only won her victory, but like the civil rights activists before her, she'd laid an important piece of groundwork for the fight ahead.

Chapter 2

Beryl, Bernice, Bunny

"Dr. Sandler has been a fierce pioneer in the movement to abolish sex discrimination in higher education due to her visionary, courageous and fearless leadership for women's rights and gender equality for more than four decades."
—APA Presidential Citation Award

During her lifetime, Dr. Bernice Sandler received over 10 honorary degrees on top of her earned doctorate, as well as numerous awards, including being inducted into the National Women's Hall of Fame in 2013. She discovered the key that would unlock women's equality in education, fought tirelessly for women's rights, and is now known as The Godmother of Title IX. But it wasn't always this way. Many years ago, she was just a girl. And everyone called her Bunny.

Bunny was born on March 3, 1928. It was cold that Saturday in Flatbush, New York, the Brooklyn neighborhood she would soon call home. Though she couldn't know it, her birthday was a notable day in women's equality for more than one reason. Not only had the Godmother of Title IX just been born, but due in part to pressure from women's groups and other activists, organizers of the famous Miss America pageant voted that very day to discontinue their competition. The pageant wouldn't begin again until 1933.

Bunny was also born on the eve of The Great Depression, a decade (1929–1939) in American history known for economic crisis. During the worst years, unemployment rose to 25%, leaving one in every four people out of work. Many were hopeless and hungry, even destitute.

Bunny's parents, Abe and Ivy Resnick, were Jewish immigrants. Abe came from a long line of rabbis in Eastern Europe, but the family wasn't very religious. The Resnicks did follow one traditional Hebrew custom though. In addition to their American names, Jewish children are often given a Hebrew name. Though Ivy had settled on Beryl as the American name for her baby, the pediatrician refused to write it on the birth certificate, actually telling her he wouldn't inflict a name like that on a child. Always a tenacious problem-solver, Ivy shrugged and quickly chose Bernice, a name she'd loved from the beginning of her pregnancy. In Yiddish, Bernice is Bunya, which quickly became Bunny.

Young Bernice was called by her nickname so often that on her first day of kindergarten she didn't recognize her own name. That morning, Bunny waited as roll was called, one name after the other, until her teacher asked, "Did I miss anyone?" Bunny raised her hand. "I'm Bunny Resnick," she announced. "No," her teacher said, "you're Bernice Resnick." Bunny burst into

Bunny (right) with her big sister Rhoda in South Fallsburg, NY, summer 1934.

tears. She hadn't known her real name was Bernice! Ivy made a quick trip to the school to explain. From that day on, Bernice was Bunny at school, too.

School, as well as the outside world, was full of sexism back then, though no one had a word for what they were experiencing. From boys hogging the big outdoor playground in elementary school, leaving girls only a small corner where they could jump rope, to boys being the only ones allowed to use the long pole that opened the high, out-of-reach school windows, Bunny didn't like it. She didn't like that girls weren't allowed to fill the inkwells, or that only boys could be crossing guards and wear the important, bright orange sash across their chests. And she especially didn't like that only boys were allowed to run the slide projector, which at the time was the height of technology. "I was very envious," she recalled.

In those days, Bunny remembered, girls were offered fashion or cooking classes, while boys enjoyed career counseling and vocational guidance. And if there was an overflow of students in a class with both boys and girls, the girls had to leave to make room for the boys. Early in her schooling, Bunny wanted to make a birdhouse like the boys in shop class, but she wasn't allowed. Instead, she had to take home economics, which meant cooking and sewing an apron. Bunny didn't want to do any of it. But like many girls and boys who didn't want to do the expected thing, she wasn't given a choice. It was simply the way the world was.

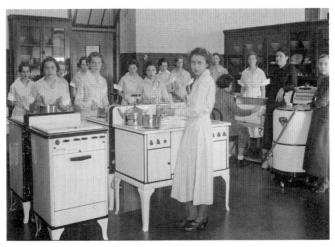

Cooking class, Bethesda-Chevy Chase High School, 1935.

Whether it was the inkwells or the slide projector, or the apron in that home economics class, Bunny Sandler recognized at a very young age that the world was full of wrongs and injustices. And she couldn't stand for it. "If you'd have asked me when I was a child, 'What do you want to do when you grow up?'" Bunny remembered, "I would've said I wanted to change the world and make it better."

Despite the challenging time, Bunny had a happy childhood. The Resnicks lived in a one-bedroom apartment full of books where she learned a love of reading and education. Her parents owned and ran a small department store called Resnick's. At the start, Resnick's sold toys, gifts, and women's clothing, but eventually focused on clothes. On Sundays the store closed early, and the family usually visited a used bookstore downtown where Bunny and her older sister Rhoda (who everyone called Ricki) were each given 15 cents to spend. By age nine Bunny was venturing to the public library on her own, always careful when she crossed the busy streets. With such a love of books, it seems no wonder Bunny became an academic. From her mother Ivy she learned the value of hard work and determination, and to follow important things through to the end. Her father Abe fostered a love of nature in Bunny that she held tight to her whole life, passing it to her own children and grandchildren as they grew.

After high school, where Bunny was predictably a good student, she chose to study psychology because she was interested in people. But it wouldn't be easy. "When I applied to college," Bunny recalled, "it was openly known that women needed higher grades and test scores in order to be accepted. No one complained—it was just the way things were." Despite the double standard, in 1948 she graduated from Brooklyn College with a BA in Psychology. Two years later she earned her MA in Clinical and School Psychology from the City College of New York. Soon after, she met Jerrold Sandler and they got married. They eventually settled in Ann Arbor, Michigan. Being married didn't stop Bunny from wanting to continue her education.

Left: Bunny and Jerry Sandler, 1952.
Right: Bunny and her daughter Emily, 1958.

But being a woman could have. Though she had excellent credentials, she wasn't accepted to any of the doctoral programs in psychology she applied to. Bunny didn't know it at the time, but many universities had quotas for how many women were admitted. When she discovered this years later, it only fueled her determination to make a difference.

Bunny's daughters Emily and Deborah, with Ivy, at Resnick's, 1962

Still, she didn't let those obstacles stand in her way. Thinking social work might be a more hospitable field for women, she began a part-time program in that department at the University of Michigan. But with two young children at home, the demands were soon too much, and she took a break from school. During these years her creative outlets became drawing and playing guitar, which she was quite good at. For a short time, she even ran a "Learn to Play Guitar" school from her home by mail. However, after a few years and a move to the Washington, DC, area in 1964, Bunny found her way back to school—though again getting in wasn't easy. Not only was she initially rejected from the University of Maryland, but the department told her very bluntly they didn't accept many women, especially older women. It was only after a lucky meeting with the Admissions Chair at a social gathering that Bunny convinced him to let her in. Finally, in 1969 she graduated with her doctorate in Counseling and Personnel Services.

Though women did experience some social progress during Bunny's childhood, especially after the Depression as President Franklin Roosevelt expanded social welfare programs and appointed women to government positions, sex discrimination was still the norm. Even in the 1960s, as Bunny was applying to doctoral programs for the first time, girls and women were still considered the "fairer" or "weaker" sex. In fact, the wrong-headed thinking about women and the devaluing of their place in society was so pervasive that when Bunny mentioned to her dissertation advisor that she'd like to study women for her project, he explained that wouldn't count as "real research" and insisted she find another topic.

That Was Legal?

page 21

The truth was, though women of color had been in the workforce for some time, experiencing both racial and gender discrimination, for the majority of White women life was still at home, as wives and mothers. And the women who did work mainly took jobs as schoolteachers, nurses, secretaries, or in some type of domestic service. Even so, many people disapproved of married women working and thought they took jobs away from men. People thought a woman's place was at home, with children who needed a full-time mother. It might be hard to imagine now, but this was the environment Bunny grew up in. Abe and Ivy, though, were strong proponents of what we now call "social justice." They taught Bunny to speak up and ask questions when something didn't seem right.

Sexist ads like this were common during Bunny's lifetime.

Because the word "sexism" didn't exist, experiencing such an unpleasant and unfair situation was frustrating. It's hard to understand something when there isn't a name for it. "You didn't even use the word 'unfair,'" Bunny remembered, "you just didn't like it." Long before, suffragists like Susan B. Anthony referred to the imbalance of power between men and women as "the oligarchy of sex," but it wouldn't be until the women's movement of the 1960s that women, and men, could put a clearer name to what had been happening. The word "sexism" helped establish a framework and gave people a more concrete way to point out and understand this type of injustice. Still, there were few, if any, conferences on women, or newsletters about women's rights or sex discrimination. This was also a time before email and the internet. Even as the women's movement progressed and sexism was beginning to be talked about, gathering and sharing information was much more challenging than today.

Growing up during the financial crisis of the 1930s made an impact on Bunny, too. "Because of the Depression," she recalled, "there was a real push to improve society as a whole." Her early inclination toward social activism and fairness, the determination and resolve she learned from Ivy, and the family's love of reading and education gave Bunny the skills and gumption she'd need for the fight ahead, to change the world like she'd always wanted.

That Was Legal?

Before Title IX, sex discrimination in education happened in lots of ways. Some were obvious or overt, while others were more subtle. Margaret Dunkle and Bunny addressed both types in a 1974 paper written to help organizations understand Title IX and follow the new regulations.

Overt examples of sex discrimination might include boy and girl students having different curfews, rules requiring boys keep short hair while girls can have long or short hair, or dress codes allowing only boys to wear pants. Other examples were expelling pregnant students and requiring the prom or homecoming queen to be a virgin.

Subtle forms of discrimination were harder to spot, but still there. Organizations establishing rigid time limits for finishing degrees, making it difficult to transfer credits, not offering a leave of absence policy, or having a requirement to live on campus are all examples of subtle sex discrimination. Margaret Dunkle and Bunny argued these school rules (and others like them) have a subtle discriminatory impact on women because of the disproportionate burden women have in raising children and caring for the family.

TRY THIS:
Do an Interview

Think about some older people in your life. For this activity, the person you choose should have been born before 1972—before Title IX became a law. This project will work with anyone of that age, but your results will probably be more striking if you interview an older woman. Maybe you're lucky enough to have a grandmother or two, a great aunt, or even a neighbor you're friendly with.

Once you've decided on a subject, brainstorm some questions. Consider asking about things that will help you understand what life was like, especially for a girl, before Title IX. You might ask your subject if she played sports. If so, which ones and what was it like? If not, why? Was it because she wasn't interested, or because sports weren't available? If she says she wasn't interested, consider following up about why she thinks that was so. You might ask what classes she took in school, and if she had any choice in the matter. If there was an automotive class in junior or senior high, would she have been allowed to participate? Were boys allowed or interested in cooking classes? If not, consider asking why she thinks that was so.

Think about your questions in advance so you're prepared, but try and be flexible during the interview. Remember, it's a friendly conversation with someone you know. Most people are delighted to share their history and will likely be honored that you're interested.

Aim for 10-15 questions, realizing you might not get to ask all of them. Once you have questions, contact your subject and set up a date and time to meet. If you're planning to record the interview, be sure to ask permission. And if possible, bring a notebook and something to write with. You'll want to take notes even if you're recording. As always, remember the essentials: who, what, when, where, why, and how. You might be surprised how many incredible stories those six little words can unlock!

Once you're finished with the interview, read through the answers. Did you learn something new about your subject? Try to imagine them as a young person. Do their answers make you understand them in a different way? Learning new things about someone in your life, while gaining valuable interview experience at the same time, can be rewarding and fun!

Chapter 3

Pandora's Box

"When I got a chance to work with people like Bunny Sandler I was just delighted. As I did whenever I encountered a real activist, I took her on as a client and pushed every legal and political button I knew."
—Vince Macaluso, former Assistant Director of the U.S. Department of Labor's compliance division

Bunny sat at her kitchen table, her heart racing with excitement. She knew she'd found the way in, that the footnote of Executive Order 11246 was the path to combat discrimination for women working in colleges and universities. But now what? She had no legal experience. She wasn't a politician or familiar with the intricacies of government. "I didn't know a thing about policies or complaints," Bunny remembered.

Luckily, she'd discovered the Women's Equity Action League (WEAL). Founded by Ohio-based attorney Elizabeth Boyer in 1968, WEAL was a national women's group devoted to helping women by lobbying for legislative change and legal actions. The group was a more

conservative spin-off of the National Organization for Women (NOW) and was designed to be conventional in its appearance and demeanor. Unlike NOW, members of WEAL didn't protest or hold rallies. But they did want equality for women. WEAL focused mainly on fighting sex discrimination in education and advancing women's economic status by fighting to change laws. Bunny had seen one of their ads in the newspaper and attended a national conference. She liked the people she'd met and what she'd heard, so she joined. As a member of WEAL, Bunny's emerging feminism began to express itself. The partnership ended up being extremely important.

When Bunny brought her bombshell discovery to WEAL, they made her Chair of the Action Committee on Federal Contract Compliance. But Bunny wasn't just the chair; it turned out she was the whole committee. At the time, WEAL didn't even have an office, though no one on the outside could tell. Bunny's new title added legitimacy to her effort in the emerging organization, which would help with her next move.

Bunny's WEAL membership card for 1975.

Acting in her newly appointed position, Bunny prepared to call the Office of Federal Contract Compliance
at the U.S. Department of Labor. But she was worried.
She doubted herself. She felt like she must've gotten
something wrong. Like many women, her confidence was low. "Surely," she thought, "someone else
would've seen this." But Ivy had taught her to ask
questions. After all, the worst they could say was no.
Bunny took a deep breath and dialed. She was trans-
ferred to the Assistant Director, Vince Macaluso, who
was aware of the footnote. "He'd been waiting for
someone to come," Bunny recalled. He was supportive
over the phone and suggested they meet at his office.
But Bunny was so unaccustomed to someone being
this interested in her work that she thought he might
be hitting on her.

She needn't have worried. Macaluso was delighted
to see her, but not because he wanted a date. He was
thrilled someone had finally noticed how the Executive
Order's expanded coverage made many common
practices by colleges and universities suddenly illegal.
Though he was sympathetic to women's equality and
preventing sex discrimination, it wasn't part of his
job to launch an investigation or file a complaint. But
he was happy to secretly help Bunny do it. "She was
a sparkplug," Macaluso remembered later. Because
he helped Bunny navigate the bureaucratic process,

kickstarted her letter-writing campaign for women in academics, and suggested she conduct a survey of sex discrimination against women employees in colleges and universities, Macaluso launched the Bunny Sandler we know today. She left his office that day invigorated, knowing she needed to gather as much information as possible.

And that's exactly what she did. As an academic scholar familiar with collecting research, Bunny was uniquely qualified to compile the needed evidence. One of her first steps was to do an informal survey at the University of Maryland. In 1969, pretending to do "academic research," Bunny asked each department for a list of its faculty. As expected, the results showed an alarming lack of women—the prestigious departments had very few women scholars, and many that were there didn't have tenure. Expanded research showed other universities with similar discriminatory issues. For example, though 25 percent of Columbia's doctorates were awarded to women, women only accounted for 2 percent of its tenured faculty. Bunny's research also demonstrated sex discrimination happening through admission quotas and salary differences. The data made one thing clear: the higher the rank, the fewer the women. Bunny's research was revealing patterns of sex discrimination in education she'd experienced firsthand.

"First Dollar" by cartoonist Doug Marlette, 1982.

She was experiencing some other things firsthand, too. Her research made her realize just how bad things had been, how all of this discrimination had been happening in the open, under all their noses, with most people not even talking about it. It had simply been accepted. But now she was waking to reality. She was understanding for the first time that people sometimes ignored you or treated you differently because you were a woman. It was "like blinders have been removed from your eyes," she recalled later, "and you say, oh my gosh!" From that moment on, Bunny's eyes were wide open.

In January of 1970, acting on behalf of WEAL, Bunny filed the first administrative class action complaint. It charged an industry-wide pattern of sex discrimination and asked for a compliance review for any college or university in the U.S. that had federal contracts. Much of the 80-page complaint was Bunny's study, illustrating discrimination through her researched, collected data. Complaints were addressed to the Secretary of Labor, but on Macaluso's advice Bunny also sent copies to members of Congress, asking them to write the Secretary of Labor, urging him to enforce the Executive Order—which was his job. This tactical move was brilliant; when the weighty report landed on congressional desks it not only put the issue of sex discrimination in education on their radar, making it part of the conversation, but it bumped the issue up the chain of command, drawing much needed attention.

Vince Macaluso and Bunny. Macaluso played little part in Title IX after helping to launch Bunny's activism, but she remained thankful, sometimes referring to him as the "Godfather of Title IX."

Not long after Bunny filed, a snippet about the complaint appeared in a periodical called the Saturday Review of Literature. After that, the flood gates opened. Word of mouth spread, and women in the academic community all over the country began sharing their stories. They sent letter after letter, all typed or hand-written, to Bunny and WEAL, outlining personal instances of discrimination. Many asked how to file or be part of the complaint.

Mostly, women wrote to say they'd been overlooked for promotions, tenure, or had their contracts terminated while the men in their department, who in many cases had less experience or were less qualified, continued to progress in their field or be promoted. But some examples were more obvious. One woman explained she'd been rejected for a position at a prestigious university with a note mentioning, "Your qualifications are excellent, but we already have a woman in this department." Another outlined difficulties a woman engineering student faced: After several weeks without access to the locker she'd been promised, which she needed to store her lab equipment and clothes, she was told she could have the locker if she really wanted it, but it was in the men's bathroom.

Through her research Bunny learned some colleges prohibited women from majoring in chemistry, or from even taking chemistry classes at all. She discovered a well-known veterinary school had an admissions quota of just two women a year, no matter how many applied or how qualified they were. She also uncovered that a prominent southern school had rejected 21,000 women for admission, and during the same period had turned down zero—literally zero—men.

And Bunny filed for them all. At that time, you didn't have to be an attorney or have a special connection to the case to file an administrative complaint with the Department of Labor. Importantly, you didn't even have to name the specific person who'd been harmed. Having solid data on statistical disparities was enough to make your case, which made many women who'd experienced discrimination more willing to send letters and speak up. With Bunny's signature on the complaints instead of their own, women were more protected from retaliation in the form of censure, loss of tenure or contracts, or even termination. By April of 1970, just four months after Bunny filed the first complaint, Department of Labor investigations into sex discrimination against women academics in American universities were actually happening. "Pandora's Box had finally been opened," she said later.

Eventually, Bunny filed about 250 complaints through WEAL. And every time a complaint was filed, members of Congress received another letter. In some cases, letters came from both the individual who'd experienced the discrimination and from Bunny, each one asking their Senators and Representatives to keep them informed on the progress of the complaint and to write the Secretary of Labor, asking him to do his job and enforce amended Executive Order 11246. "We generated so much Congressional mail," Bunny recalled, "that the Departments of Labor, and Health, Education and Welfare had to assign several full-time personnel to handle the letters." Not only that, but women's organizations other than WEAL began doing the same.

Bunny at work, 1971.

Representative Edith Green, a Democrat from Oregon, was a member of WEAL's Advisory Board and had received copies of Bunny's complaints to the Secretary of Labor. Green also chaired the Special Sub-committee on Education for the Committee on Education and Labor and had been working to end sex discrimination in education for a long time. And even though sex discrimination was prohibited by the amended Executive Order Bunny had found, it wasn't law. It could be easily changed or removed by the next president or administration if they wanted. Green wanted something more permanent to prevent sex discrimination in education. But she had no constituency yet, no actual data to support her claims or people to testify at a congressional hearing.

Bunny's research changed all that. The stories and hard data she'd collected from women in colleges and universities across the country were exactly what Green needed. And on Wednesday, June 17, 1970, Representative Edith Green introduced a bill (Section 805 of HR 16098) to address sex discrimination in education. Armed with Bunny's research and suggested witnesses, Green convened the first congressional hearings on sex discrimination in education in the U.S. House of Representatives.

TRY THIS:

Write Your Representatives

You probably already know that in the United States we elect politicians to represent us to the government. Congress is part of the legislative branch and has two parts: the Senate and the House of Representatives. Each state elects two Senators to represent them, but the number of Representatives a state elects is based on its population. For example, California, a state with a very large population, elects 53 representatives, while Alaska, a state with a much smaller population, elects only one.

Each state has its own government, too, led by the Governor. People vote to send elected representatives to serve and advocate for them in state government, to consider enacting new laws, balance budgets, and even hold impeachment hearings, much like in the federal government.

All of which means that right now as you're reading these words, there are at least 3–4 people whose actual job is to represent YOU to the state or federal government*. For real. That's kind of exciting when you think about it! And powerful. And while you might be too young to vote right now, you're never too young to get informed—and involved.

As a first step, try investigating who your state and federal representatives are. Don't forget, Senators (both state and federal) are representatives too. A quick Google search or a resource like govtrak.us should do the trick. Spend a few minutes learning about the people who have been elected to represent you. Where do they come from? Do they live near you or far away? Are they familiar and involved in your community? What do they stand for? Do you feel a connection, or like you have shared values? Do you feel like they actually do represent you, or not? If you bumped into them on the street, what would you want them to know about you and your life? How could they help YOU?

Once you have a basic understanding of who your representatives are and what they stand for, think about issues that are important to you. Maybe you're passionate about the environment, veterans' rights, or making sure anti-racist history and curriculums are being taught in your school. Maybe it's more specific, like making sure the roads near your home are properly maintained so you can stop smacking your head every time the bus hits all those potholes. Chances are, no matter what social issue you care about, your representative has a position on it. If you don't like their position—or even if you do—call or write and let them know. Express yourself as a citizen in their district. Contact information like office locations, email, websites, and phone numbers is readily available. Remember, representatives are exactly that—their job is to represent you. Your job, if you choose to accept it, is to stay informed and hold them accountable.

*A notable exception is the District of Columbia, otherwise known as Washington, DC. Residents of the District do not have true representation in Congress. Residents elect a non-voting delegate to the House of Representatives and two shadow Senators to the Senate. But those Congress members cannot vote on legislation. Furthermore, the District does not operate autonomously like a state and does not have a Governor. This means that the District government is not allowed to manage its own local affairs and truly represent the wishes of people living and working there. If you're ever in DC, you may notice that nearly every vehicle protests this injustice.

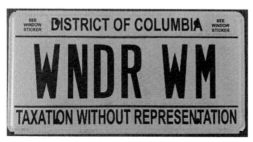

Bunny was passionate about the fight for Washington, DC, statehood and proudly displayed this license plate.

Chapter 4

Girls Just Want to Have... Hearings

"[Title IX] was perhaps the most important legislation for women since the 19th Amendment right to vote. Every woman who has gone to college, gotten a law degree or a medical degree, was able to take shop instead of home-ec, or went to a military academy really owes [Bunny] a huge debt."—Margaret Dunkle, close colleague and friend of Bunny Sandler

On June 17, 1970, Representative Edith Green called the first hearings on sex discrimination in education to order. Bunny Sandler had a lot on the line. Not only were the hearings largely based on her research, but she'd helped organize them. And she'd suggested nearly all the witnesses, pulling from her widening knowledge of interested individuals and women's advocacy groups forming around the country. Plus, she had to testify. She'd come a long way from the day she'd had to convince herself to call Vince Macaluso.

After welcoming everyone, Representative Green gave a brief overview of facts, demonstrating the need for change. "Let us not deceive ourselves," she said. "Our educational institutions have proven to be no bastions of democracy." Women, she explained, made up less than 10% of full professors in the country. At the time, only 8% of U.S. scientists were women. Physicians claimed 6.7% percent, lawyers had 3.5%, and only 1% of engineers in America were women. "While the United States prides itself on being a leader of nations," Green stated, "it has been backward in its treatment of its working women."

Witnesses, mostly women, cited numerous studies in their testimony. Some addressed the inaccuracy of common misconceptions about working women, like women only work to earn spending money, or women quit working after they get married. In reality, studies showed women worked to support themselves or their families, and nearly 60% of working women were married. In addition, a 1970 U.S. News and World Report included in the record noted that women were being "protected" out of better, higher paying jobs. For example, at the time many states had

37 Words
page 47

40

laws prohibiting women from working more than eight hours at a time, preventing them from being eligible for higher-level jobs that required overtime. Some states also had laws restricting the amount of weight a woman could lift at work, again showing these "protections" actually limited women's opportunities. Men, of course, had no such restrictions.

A representative of the American Civil Liberties Union (ACLU) testified at the hearing, speaking about the intersection of Black people and women, and about how the oppression people face because of their race was similar in some ways to the repression of women. She also explained how Black women are doubly discriminated against.

When it was Bunny's time to testify, she came out swinging. Though the air conditioning was making the room uncomfortably cold, the scorching case she presented must've warmed things up. "Half of the brightest people in this country—half of the most talented people with the potential for the highest intellectual endeavor are women. These women will encounter discrimination after discrimination as they try to use their talents in the university world. They will be discriminated against when they first apply for admission. They will be discriminated against when they apply for financial and scholarship aid. They will be discriminated against when they apply for positions on the faculty. If they are hired, they will be promoted far more slowly than their male counterparts; and furthermore, if hired at all, women will most likely receive far less money than their male colleagues. And all of this is legal!"

Bunny continued, methodically presenting evidence, showing the patterns of discrimination she'd uncovered. She explained that unofficial quotas existed in many professional and graduate schools, that girls needed higher grades for admission at many colleges and universities, and that "as faculty, women can look forward to low pay, low status, and little or no opportunity for promotion, and even difficulty in finding employment." She pointed out how common ads at the time, like "Engineer, male only," "Geologist, male only," or "Secretary, female only" that recruited for government and corporate employers in college periodicals were problematic and clearly in violation of amended Executive Order 11246. Examples continued, systematically presenting the case of sex discrimination in education throughout her testimony. One university's publication for undergraduate admission stated, "Admission of women on the freshman level will be restricted to those who are especially well qualified." Bunny then noted the 1970 freshman class for that university showed 1893 men and just 426 women.

She testified that many schools discouraged part-time study, especially for graduate students, and explained how that effectively punished women trying to balance professional training with family responsibilities. Her testimony included that, disturbingly, in 1970 the percentage of women earning MDs was the same as it had been in the 1920s.

Left: Male Only/Female Only Want Ads in The Washington Times, 1915.
Right: Poster created by Albert M. Bender for the WPA between 1936 and 1941.

Bunny also made clear that her research was legitimate. "Let me add here that none of WEAL's filing have been based on anecdotal material; about 20 have been based on discriminatory advertising; the remainder and majority of the complaints have been based on hard statistical data. As more and more information has been collected, there is no question whatsoever that there is a massive, consistent and vicious pattern of sex discrimination in our universities and colleges."

In addition to the witnesses Bunny had suggested, other organizations having an interest in educational issues were expected to attend. At the time, The American Council on Education kept track of legislation that might have an impact on colleges and universities. But their lobbyist decided not to participate, claiming, "There is no sex discrimination in education," and "even if there was, it wasn't a problem."

The truth was, many people agreed with him. The issue of sex discrimination in education was getting some attention, but for the most part Representative Green's hearings flew completely under the radar. In fact, few of the men on Green's subcommittee bothered to attend for the entire time, choosing instead to drop by here and there. And while the newly established Chronicle of Higher Education (which later became the newspaper of record for higher education) was represented by reporter Cheryl Fields, no major newspaper covered the seven days of hearings. "Hardly anyone outside the Congress was following it except for some women's organizations," Bunny recalled. And the few "who did know about the bill," she continued, "did not believe it would have any meaningful impact."

However, the hearings were a success. Not only had Bunny's data and the witness testimonies supported the need for Green's proposed bill, which would eventually become Title IX of the Educational Amendments of 1972, but no one from the opposition even bothered to show up. That absence allowed seven days of Congressional hearings, where day after day witnesses provided testimony and hard statistical data concerning the inequities and injustice of a sexist system, to go nearly unnoticed by the opposition, with no rebuttal or disagreement entered on the record.

When it was all over, Representative Green hired Bunny to compile the written record of the hearings. "Thus," Bunny remembered, "I became the first person ever appointed to the staff of a Congressional Committee to work specifically on women's issues." The final report for all seven days of testimony and evidence supporting sex discrimination in education was a two-volume set, totaling nearly 1300 pages. Nothing like it had ever been published before. "It was an eye opener for anyone who saw it," Bunny said.

The hearings added legitimacy to the issue of sex discrimination in education and gave the bill momentum. By the next year, Senator Birch Bayh, a Democrat from Indiana, championed Title IX as an amendment to a larger education bill. Around this time, Bunny and a small group of activists went to Representative Green, offering to vocally support the bill. But Green worried drawing attention to the issue would do more harm than good. "She was adamant that we not do any lobbying whatsoever," Bunny remembered. "We were very skeptical of her reasoning but had to listen to her, and of course, she was right."

POLITICAL POWE

page 48

Bunny (center) and colleagues with Senator Birch Bayh (right).

After some negotiation, the bill passed the following year. Title IX was signed into law by President Richard Nixon on June 23, as part of the Education Amendments of 1972.

37 Words

"No person in the United States shall, on the basis of sex, be excluded from participation in, be denied the benefits of, or be subjected to discrimination under any educational program or activity receiving Federal financial assistance."

Title IX is a federal civil rights law based on language in Title VI of the Civil Rights Law of 1964. Title IX protects people from sex discrimination in any federally funded educational institution. Almost all schools and universities in the U.S. receive federal money. Title IX was passed as part of the Education Amendments of 1972 and became law on June 23 of that year.

All students, faculty, and employees are protected from sex discrimination and sexual harassment in education under Title IX. Students who live off campus or are assaulted at a school-sponsored event off campus are also protected by Title IX. Retaliation against someone who makes a complaint is explicitly forbidden under Title IX and counts as its own violation.

In some ways, Title IX is like Bunny Sandler—it may be small, but it carries a big punch. Contained in the one sentence core provision of that law are not only the hopes and dreams for educational equality of generations of women and girls in the United States, but the legal right to access those dreams.

Political Power

Representative Edith Green: After being an educator for 11 years, Green became the second woman to represent Oregon in the U.S. House of Representatives. She served in the House from 1955–1975, winning each of her elections with relative ease. Her continued interest in educational rights and her expertise in educational policy earned her the name Mrs. Education. Because of her groundbreaking 1970 hearings that laid the groundwork for Title IX, and championing what became Title IX for inclusion in the Education Amendments of 1972, Edith Green is now known as The Mother of Title IX.

Senator Birch Bayh: A Democrat from Indiana, Bayh served in the U.S. Senate for three terms, from 1963–1981. While there, he was involved in many groundbreaking legislative efforts, including the 1964 Civil Rights Act and the 1965 Voting Rights Act. Bayh was also the chief Senate sponsor of the Equal Rights Amendment, which passed in Congress but has yet to be ratified and adopted. He was the author and chief sponsor of Title IX in the Senate and is known as The Father of Title IX.

Representative Patsy Mink: After serving in the Hawaiian State Senate, Mink was elected as a Democrat to the U.S. House of Representatives in 1965, only a few years after Hawaii became a state. She was the first woman of color to be elected to Congress, serving from 1965 to 1977 and again from 1989 to 2003. She was the lead sponsor of the 1974 Women's Educational Equity Act, a grant program that followed Title IX to promote equal educational opportunity for women. In the years after Title IX's passage, Mink fought those who tried to water down Title IX coverage and exempt college athletics. After her death in 2002, Title IX was renamed the Patsy T. Mink Equal Opportunity in Education Act.

TRY THIS:

Conduct an Experiment

Bunny's report on sexual harassment and discrimination in education gave Representative Edith Green exactly what she needed to conduct congressional hearings. Importantly, as Bunny noted, the report wasn't based on anecdotal stories, but instead on solid research and scientifically collected data. Bunny used the scientific method to gather her information. She observed the world around her and formed a hypothesis. She investigated, gathered facts from her environment, and tested those facts against her hypothesis.

Your turn! Using the scientific method, conduct an experiment. Think about the social situations you find yourself in. It could be math class or a favorite restaurant or track practice, or anything you do regularly. Now pick one to investigate. Once you've decided, carefully observe the dynamics and interactions of the social situation until you have enough information to form a hypothesis, or theory. In Bunny's case, her experience in and observation of the world of higher education led her to the hypothesis that gender discrimination existed. Maybe your hypothesis is that watching scary movies causes people to eat more candy or popcorn than when they're watching another type of movie, like a comedy or a love story.

In this case, your data collection would involve observing the snack behavior of movie-watchers over a certain period. Keep notes of the interesting interactions on your phone or in a notebook. Try and be as systematic as possible. The information you collect during your observation period will become the evidence that will test your hypothesis!

Once you've collected your data, plug it into a simple chart or graph. Seeing data presented in a new way like this can help remove bias and paint a truer picture. Study your chart. What does your collected data tell you about your hypothesis? Does it support it? If so, consider writing a report to share your informal findings. If not, examine your experiment for variables you hadn't considered. For example, were the movie watchers hungry or full before arriving? How might that affect your data? Were the movie watchers alone or with friends? Was it the same each time? In formal experiments, scientists must consider and try to control variables like these, as they can affect the outcome.

It's also important to leave room for the possibility that regardless of variables, the data might not support your hypothesis—and that's perfectly okay. Data is impersonal. That's kind of the point. Whether your hypothesis is disproved or proved, or even if your results are inconclusive, congratulations! You've just conducted a perfectly valid informal experiment and gotten a glimpse into the scientific method.

Chapter 5

Rules of the Road

"Title IX turned out to be the legislative equivalent of a Swiss Army knife. It gave us tools to tackle all kinds of discrimination. Bunny Sandler was such a powerhouse— she changed the lives of millions of women and girls, LGBT students, and boys and men as well."
—Marty Langelan, an expert on harassment and longtime friend of Dr. Sandler

Because of the hard work and struggle of many activists, including Bunny Sandler, Title IX was finally law. They'd made it illegal for educational institutions that accepted money from the federal government to discriminate on the basis of sex. But what were the new rules K-12 schools and colleges and universities were supposed to follow? And what happened if they didn't comply? What would be the consequences?

For one, most schools could no longer use quota systems for admissions. And classes that "protected" women and girls from participating for their own good—for instance, not allowing women in a juvenile justice course to work with men offenders, or keeping girls from auto mechanics because the boys used bad language, which Bunny's daughter Emily experienced firsthand—were now illegal. Schools would now have to provide equitable treatment between girls and boys for counseling, housing, scholarships, and recruitment, just to name a few. But what about things like gym class? Would locker rooms have to be integrated? Would schools have to sponsor a girls' wrestling team, or offer cheerleading for boys? Come to think of it, many were beginning to wonder, what did all of this mean for sports in general?

In 1974, Bunny was serving as Director of the Project on the Status and Education of Women (PSEW), an organization developed under the Association of American Colleges and Universities that advocated for gender equity in education. Bunny asked the Associate Director of the PSEW, Margaret Dunkle, to research how Title IX would affect college sports. The resulting national study became the first to document and address the inequity women faced in college athletics. Paired with a landmark article published by Dunkle and Sandler that same year, much-needed guidelines and suggestions for how schools could improve and comply with Title IX were finally available. Of course, it took a while for the government to catch up and publish official regulations.

Dunkle's first report uncovered glaring examples of sex discrimination and inequity in college sports, similar to what Bunny had found in higher education. For example, some schools prohibited men and women from taking certain classes. One school didn't allow women in wrestling, or men in volleyball or self-defense. Others allowed women to satisfy gym credits by taking bowling, archery, or square dancing, but men couldn't do the same. Some schools had different, gender-based requirements for the same field of study. One college required women physical education majors to complete a service course each semester, but men had no similar requirement. Even graduation requirements varied by gender. The report showed one school demanded women show proficiency in two sports to graduate, while men needed only one.

MYTH MEETS FACT

page 63

Many schools provided trainers to men athletes, but not to women. Coaches of men's teams were usually salaried, while coaches of women's teams tended to be unpaid volunteers. Men's teams were more likely to get new equipment or uniforms, then pass their old hand-me-downs to the women. At one university, women gymnasts had no budget for athletic tape and had no choice but to wrap up with sweaty tape the men's team had already used. Many schools provided elaborate locker rooms and facilities for men, but had nothing comparable for the women, forcing them to change in their dorms or wherever they could. Some schools gave academic credit to men for playing sports, but not to women. Team doctors and medical insurance were frequently provided for men's teams to cover injuries, but, of course, not to women. The report even mentioned a women's coach who asked to borrow ice from the men's coach for an injured athlete. Instead of sharing the ice, he suggested the injured woman "put her foot in the toilet and keep flushing it." One university had over a million dollars budgeted for men's varsity sports, but none for the women. Women athletes at that school often sold apples at football games to pay for their expenses and travel. "Try to imagine a football team having a bake sale to pay for shoulder pads," Bunny noted. All of these practices, and many more shown in both groundbreaking reports done for the PSEW, were in direct violation of Title IX. And, finally, against the law.

Ironing out the details of how to solve these issues took years. It wasn't until 1975 that regulations outlining requirements for institutions to comply with the law were issued. "Getting Title IX passed," Bunny remembered, "was really the easy part." For many, that work paled in comparison to the uphill climb of developing guidelines and enforcing compliance. Margaret Dunkle's reports helped pave the way.

In the end, schools and organizations were expected to monitor themselves by appointing a Title IX Coordinator, which was actually Bunny's idea. In part, Coordinators work to maintain equity and ensure their school complies with the law. If a violation happens, it's also their job to help coordinate the investigation and disciplinary process if necessary. Students, faculty, coaches, and other community members can file complaints. Importantly, even today, complaints remain anonymous, and it is specifically forbidden for institutions to retaliate. If schools do not follow the law, they risk losing their federal funding. It is worth noting that many institutions, even now, are not in compliance, but none have ever lost funding. However, if the school is sued in court, they may be responsible to pay fines and damages.

Generally speaking, just as educational institutions could not legally categorize people by race, after 1972 it was no longer legal for them to categorize people by sex either. Including girls and women equitably in classes, extracurricular activities, and opportunities was not only expected, but required. The law said equity between women and men must be established. But that didn't mean they'd have to share the exact same facilities. As long as the girls' locker room was just as nice and well-equipped as the boys', the new law was satisfied. Still, some worried football teams, for example, would have to be gender integrated, or that they might lose valuable dollars to other less popular programs. Though this was never the case, there was a sustained effort by the athletic establishment of the time, including proposed legislation, to exempt athletics from Title IX and weaken the law in general. None of these attempts succeeded.

No one, including Bunny, knew what the ramifications of the new law would be. "Even those of us intimately involved in Title IX, such as myself," Bunny remembered later, "did not fully understand its impact at the time." Though the focus of Title IX was equal opportunity for women and girls in education, the ripple effects were enormous.

TAKING ONE FOR THE TEAM
page 67

One of those first ripples was felt in the late 1970s, when students and one faculty member at Yale sued the university (Alexander v. Yale). They argued their education and work environment was negatively affected because of sexual harassment on campus, claiming a violation of Title IX. The case went all the way to the Supreme Court. Though the students ultimately lost the case, they did get the court to acknowledge for the first time that sexual harassment was an impediment to education. This was a big step for the little law. Media coverage brought needed exposure to the issue of sexual harassment, making it more widely talked about. Soon Yale created a system for students to file complaints, and many other institutions did the same. It wasn't until 1992 that the Supreme Court ruled (Franklin v. Gwinnett) that students subjected to sexual harassment could sue for monetary damages under Title IX. And in 2011, the Obama administration issued guidelines making it clear that Title IX's protections covered sexual violence or harassment, including student to student harassment.

The Obama administration's interpretation and guidelines for Title IX also extended protection to LGBTQ+ students, stating that complaints and harass-ment due to stereotypical notions of femininity and masculinity would be investigated. This included honoring transgender and gender-nonconforming students' chosen names and pronouns, and their use of bathrooms or locker rooms aligned with their chosen gender identity. In 2017, the Trump administration rescinded those protections, claiming that "sex" protected under Title IX should be defined as a person's biological sex assigned at birth, and not their chosen gender. And under the direction of then Secretary of Education Betsy DeVos, the administration enacted changes in how Title IX cases would be interpreted. These changes included a narrowed definition of what constitutes sexual harassment, allowing cross-examination of both parties during a hearing, and raising the standard of proof needed to convict someone of a violation.

Early in its tenure, the Biden administration ordered a comprehensive review of Title IX. Some areas under consideration include how formal or informal the methods of violation notification should be, what standard of evidence will be used, and whether LGBTQ+ students should be protected by Title IX. Though a June 2020 decision by the Supreme Court redefined an old definition of "sex" to include LGBTQ+ people, giving them protection under Title VII of the Civil Rights Act of 1964, restrictions imposed by the Trump administration explicitly excluded LGBTQ+

students from Title IX protection. The Biden administration is expected to roll back these restrictions and reinstate LGBTQ+ students as a protected group under Title IX in May 2022.

Title IX not only opened the floodgates of educational and athletic opportunities for women and girls, acting, as Bunny once said, "as a shock wave on the educational establishment," but over the last 50 years the law has expanded in ways she likely never imagined. Today, Title IX is front and center in conversations about not just sports, but gender-neutral bathrooms, the #MeToo movement, and sexual assault and harassment violations in sports, schools, and workplaces. The law has had an undeniable impact on the lives of countless women and girls, boosting the confidence and self-esteem of millions. But there is still much to be done.

Bunny (far left) in a meeting with Walter Mondale (far right), the 42nd Vice President.

Ten years ago, after 40 years of Title IX, a study by the National Coalition for Women and Girls in Education (NCWGE) found students who are pregnant or have children were still struggling to not have their educational needs ignored. Sexual harassment was still an ongoing problem at all grade levels, and girls and women were still underrepresented in STEM fields.

A more recent study published in the Journal of the American Medical Association (JAMA) found women hold only 11.2% of head team physician positions in college sports. And at the same level only 31.7% of head athletic trainers are women. These statistics indicate organizational and social barriers still faced by women in the sports medicine field. Surprisingly, women's coaching opportunities have declined since Title IX passed as well. In 1972, women coached more than 90 percent of women's teams. By 2012 that number had fallen to around 43 percent. Only 3 percent of men's teams are coached by women.

NATIONAL WOMEN'S LAW CENTER

page 68

In addition, girls may be playing more sports, but coverage of women's sports on TV is still sexist. Researchers at USC found that while women's sports air more than in past years, length of segments featuring women athletes may be shorter than those featuring men. The content of the coverage is also less exciting than the men's sports segments. Commentators tend to joke more and praise women athletes less, leading to a lackluster segment, which can seem boring. All of which means TV viewers, including young girls and women, may be getting the message that women's sports are boring.

Even more troubling, the social benefits of Title IX haven't been experienced equally. While 75% of White girls now play sports, the numbers are significantly lower for BIPOC girls. Girls of color face multiplying forces of discrimination, because of their gender and also because of their race. Opportunities are narrowed even further if they attend a mostly non-White school. "By not providing girls of color with equal opportunities to play sports," a study by the National Women's Law Center found, "schools are denying them the health, academic, and economic benefits that accompany participation."

OLYMPIC WOMEN

page 70

Like many at the time, Bunny didn't realize what ripple effects the new law might have. But in later years she recognized the achievement for what it was, and how long the fight would be. "This is not

TITLE IX STATS

page 66

just a women's movement. It is not just a feminist movement. It is a worldwide revolution which will take generations to fulfill and will have as much impact on the world as the industrial revolution has had."

Title IX remains at the heart of current social issues and policy. Whatever happens with the law in the coming years, all races and genders were meant to benefit. And though the law was primarily passed to stop discrimination against women, it protects men too. "It's an organizing tool," Bunny recalled, "to get people to think about gender."

Myth Meets Fact

Margaret Dunkle debunked many commonly held myths about female bodies and athletics in the groundbreaking report she prepared for Bunny and the PSEW in 1974. Some included:

Myth: Vigorous physical activity can make females sterile or damage their reproductive organs.
Fact: Exercise helps strengthen muscles in the pelvic area. In addition, the uterus is very shock resistant and much more protected than male genitalia.

Myth: Females can't perform at peak physical form during their period.
Fact: Athletes of all kinds, including Olympians, have won competitions and broken records during many different stages of menstruation.

Myth: Female bones are more fragile than male bones.
Fact: Females, on average, have smaller bones than males. But smaller doesn't mean weaker.

Myth: Playing sports can damage females' breasts.
Fact: Breasts can be easily protected, just like male genitalia.

Title IX Stats

Before Title IX was passed, many institutions didn't have funding for girls' sports. Only 1 in 27 girls played sports. Today it's 2 in 5. That's almost half. Because of funding and institutional opportunities—in short, because of Title IX—women competing in college sports increased 545%, and women and girls playing sports in high school increased 990%. All since 1972.

Title IX's impact goes beyond women enjoying sports and extracurricular activities though. Studies show women and girls who play sports have fewer health issues, stay in school longer, and are more likely to find quality jobs. Importantly, they are also more likely to become leaders.

But there's still plenty to be done. Girls of color didn't experience benefits from Title IX at the same rate White girls did. And they still don't. Studies show girls of color are less likely to participate in athletics, keeping them from enjoying the important social, health, and personal benefits of sports. Active involvement on the federal, state, and local level is needed to remedy the issue.

In addition, lower levels of education (K-12) are still behind colleges and universities when it comes to awareness and enforcement of Title IX issues. Segregating students based on gender or encouraging "boy" interests and "girl" interests can encourage the problem. Changes on this level, Bunny noted, "are weaker, less frequent, less extensive and less well done." This may be because older students are more aware of sexual harassment and discrimination and may be more likely to file a complaint.

Taking One for the Team

In 1976, 19 women from Yale's varsity rowing team stripped naked, wrote TITLE IX on their backs and chests and marched into the athletic director's office to protest the lack of shower facilities for the women's team.

Chris Ernst in Director of Physical Education Joni Barnett's office at Yale, protesting gender inequity.

Team captain Chris Ernst led the protest. Though Title IX had been law since 1972, many organizations lagged in implementing the changes. Instead of proper facilities, like a locker room and warm showers at the boathouse as the men's team enjoyed, a team of nearly 30 women shared a one-person bathroom and a small, portable changing area. Rowing practice often left the athletes damp and cold, but the women couldn't clean up or get warm until after a drafty bus ride to campus, followed by a quick dinner before the dining hall closed. Despite this, they were still highly ranked in the national championships.

"These are the bodies Yale is exploiting," Ernst read in her statement to the director. When the story was picked up by the national media, word quickly spread. By the following year the women's rowing team at Yale had a locker room.

National Women's Law Center

Formed in 1972 by Nancy Duff Campbell and Marcia D. Greenberger, the National Women's Law Center has been fighting for gender justice for half a century. Using legal and public policy as well as the court system, the NWLC works for gender justice, centering those that experience social inequity the most. The Center believes that "justice for her is justice for all."

In its early days, the Center focused on reproductive rights. They helped stop the coercive use of an experimental contraceptive on poor and institutionalized women. They also secured regulations to keep poor women from being sterilized involuntarily. And because of an NWLC win in 2011, contraception and women's well visits are now included in preventative care under the Affordable Care Act. Further, the Center helped establish new state laws stating that employers have to accommodate pregnant women to help them stay on the job.

Protecting and enforcing Title IX is a priority, too. In 1977 the Center won a battle compelling the government to enforce Title IX's hard-won regulations in a timely manner. And they've kept up the fight. More recently, the Center filed a brief in support of a trans-inclusive athletic policy under the requirements of Title IX, and an appeal on behalf of a student survivor of sexual assault.

From supporting transgender women and girls in their fight for recognition and equity, to the #MeToo movement, to the Center's pivotal role in the long battle to end the ban on women in ground combat in the military, the NWLC has been, and remains, front and center in the fight for gender equity. https://nwlc.org/

Olympic Women

1896: Athens, Greece, hosts the first modern Olympic Games. But women aren't allowed to participate.

1900: Women compete in the Olympics for the first time. Twenty-two out of 997 total athletes are women. They participate in tennis, golf, equestrianism, croquet, and sailing during the games in Paris, France.

1960: Sports like gymnastics and track and field have opened to women, though stipulations exist requiring their shorts to be no more than 4 inches above the knee.

1998: The International Olympic Committee (IOC) decides all new sports must include women's events.

2016: Women make up 45% of athletes in the summer games in Rio de Janeiro, Brazil. But other numbers remain low. Only 10-11% of coaches at the Olympics are women.

2019: Women's leadership roles behind the scenes of the Olympics increased over the years, though still only 36.7% of the International Olympic Committee's commissions are chaired by women.

TRY THIS:

Find Your Title IX Coordinator

One of the rules established by Title IX states that every public school, from K-12 to college and beyond, is required to have at least one employee who's designated to coordinate the school's compliance with Title IX—to make sure the school is following the law. That person is usually called the Title IX coordinator. Simply put, if the school takes federal funds, they need to have a Title IX coordinator.

To make sure the school is following the rules, a Title IX coordinator has to have a strong understanding of the law. It's their job to ensure that a procedure for filing a grievance or complaint is established and in place. That procedure should be public and easily accessible. If a student or parent wants to file a complaint, it's the Title IX coordinator's job to help facilitate that, and to coordinate the investigation and potential disciplinary process. Retaliation by schools against someone filing a complaint is expressly forbidden. The coordinator should help make sure that part of the law is observed, too. Many coordinators will also develop programs within the school or district to educate employees, students, and community members about Title IX rights and regulations. These programs can raise awareness about gender discrimination and help decrease incidents at schools. Title IX coordinators should work to ensure a fair process for everyone involved.

Let's find yours! Hopefully you'll never need your Title IX coordinator, but it's good to know who they are just in case. It's also good to make sure your school is complying with the law. A quick internet search of your school or district should give you the information. Coordinators are usually found under policies, regulations, or maybe non-discrimination notices. Contact information like email or phone numbers should be public and easy to find. Once you've found the contact person, make a note of it in case you ever need it.

If you can't find a Title IX coordinator for your school, you may want to contact a trusted teacher, the principal or head of school, or someone on the school board. It may seem intimidating, but you have a legal right to this information. Questions to ask might include:

◊ *Do we have a Title IX coordinator?*

◊ *If so, why is their information so hard to find? If not, we need one. Gender discrimination in education is unacceptable and against the law.*

Students protesting their school's mishandling of sexual violence at graduation.

Chapter 6

Chilly Climate

"Dr. Bernice Sandler leaves behind an extraordinary legacy. She spent decades fighting for our rights to learn, to teach, to be seen as equals—and the landmark legislation she helped pass began a new era for women in this country."
—Melinda Gates

During the long process to establish regulations for Title IX, Bunny realized the fight for women's equity in higher education was going to take longer than she'd imagined. "I used to think it would take five years to get it all taken care of," she recalled. "Now I think it will take hundreds of years." And though sex discrimination in education was now illegal, the patterns her research had uncovered, making Edith Green's hearings in the summer of 1970 possible, were more like low-hanging fruit than the whole diseased tree. Once you looked past the overt examples Bunny had found, it soon became clear that deeply rooted beliefs and systems were still in place, affording preferential treatment to men in education. Bunny dedicated the rest of her life to exposing and upending those systems.

Years later at a conference, Bunny noticed women kept being interrupted. And, she realized, it was happening to them much more often than to the men. Being a curious researcher, she pulled some paper from her bag and began an informal observational survey. She documented the women being interrupted at twice the rate as men. When she mentioned the behavior to the organizers, they denied it, suggesting she'd misunderstood or counted wrong. But the next day none of the women were interrupted. The organizers may not have taken her seriously to her face, but something was different. Bunny was hooked. Not only was the phenomenon interesting, but the behavior seemed changeable. She had her next project.

Having lived through an era of sexism without words to express the experience, being able to name a phenomenon was especially important to Bunny. By 1982, along with co-author Roberta Hall, Bunny had written the definitive paper on what became known as the "Chilly Climate." If you're a woman or from a minority group and have ever felt unwelcome at school or work but couldn't put your finger on why, you may have experienced what Bunny described.

The research leading to the paper, done for the PSEW, showed the subtle ways men and women students are treated differently in classrooms, by both men and women professors. For example, men are called on more often than women, and in general speak more in class. Teachers respond more to comments from men than to comments from women. When they do speak, women are interrupted more often than men, both by faculty and other students. Notably, men tend to interrupt more than women, too. Bunny and Hall's research also showed that when women are called on, sometimes they're referred to by their physical appearance, such as "blonde," instead of by their names. Perhaps more insidious, the paper pointed out both women and men faculty members may unknowingly make eye contact with only men students when looking for an answer—a subtle sign to everyone in the room that the women aren't expected to respond.

In addition, a chilly climate often involves teachers or professors devaluing women as a group during class. This might look like professors adopting an attentive posture or leaning in when a man speaks but leaning back or even looking at the clock when a woman speaks. Using examples where men are consistently shown as professionals while women are clients fits this mold, too. Men being called by their last names while women are called by their first names can have an effect as well. The behavior establishes a less formal or less valuable relationship with the women, devaluing them to everyone in the room. These subtle forms of sex discrimination may be unintentional. The teacher might have an inherent bias, meaning one they aren't aware of. Even with years of work on the subject, Bunny experienced this. To some extent, we all do. In a 2013 speech on chilly climate Bunny mentioned that men get more attention of all kinds. And everyone, including herself, makes more eye contact with men. "I do this sort of automatically," she noted. "I have to say to myself, 'Look at the women as well, and not only at the men.'"

Even if unintentional, if left unchecked the results are still damaging. Both men and women internalize these subtle signals. Women may begin to reevaluate themselves, often questioning their competence. This can lead to women students losing confidence or doubting themselves. They might wonder if their opinions really matter or if their contributions are worthy after all. They may lessen their participation in class or even stop completely. Bunny and Hall showed these effects can throw women off course in their studies or career. Men are affected as well. The subtle signals may give them an inflated, and false, sense of their importance. Though Bunny is often given credit for coining the phrase "chilly climate" to describe these situations, she remained humble, pointing out that coming up with the name was a collaborative effort.

Under Bunny's leadership, the PSEW wasn't only concerned with the chilly climate for undergraduate women, but for women of color in academic institutions in particular, and for students outside of the classroom, too. The group did research on women faculty, administrators, and graduate students, and eventually included work on student-to-student harassment.

During the 1990's Bunny and researchers from the PSEW found that students who were men treated all women, including faculty, differently. For example, students who brought ideas and expectations of traditional gender roles and stereotypes to the classroom might expect women faculty to be nurturing, supportive, and motherly, or more ready to allow extra time for a project. When that didn't happen, students got upset. In fact, both men and women students became angrier at professors who were women than professors who were men who behaved in the same way. And this type of discrimination gets even more complicated. Because the learned expectation for intellectual speech is strong, assertive, and traditionally "masculine," women faculty who did behave in the traditional "feminine" pattern faced something called a double bind. Today, we call this the Likeability Trap. If women were nurturing, supportive, and motherly, they risked being seen as weaker, as not a strong intellect, and ultimately as not a good teacher. In essence, no matter what they did, they couldn't win. All of these subtle patterns, Bunny said, "gave a powerful message to women and men that women were outsiders to the academic enterprise."

In later years, Bunny expanded her work to studying sexual harassment in education. She spoke frequently on the subject at colleges and universities and enjoyed sharing her findings, especially with young people. Sexual harassment, she pointed out, was a continuum—from an off-color joke or an unwelcome hand on the shoulder to the crime of sexual assault. Unwanted attention, especially when it happens between people with different levels of power, like a student and teacher or an employee and boss, is harassment. And while Title IX is a civil rights law, it still protects people from sexual harassment in education.

LIKEABILITY TRAP
page 87

Bunny's research found that sexual harassment, like a chilly climate, also traps girls and women in a double bind. Is that creepy hand on her shoulder purposeful, or just an accident? Should she ignore the behavior, which could give the mistaken impression she's enjoying it, or should she report it and risk being seen as a "bad sport"? Worse, reporting the behavior might end up with her not being taken seriously or believed at all. What is the risk of retaliation? Might she lose her job or a recommendation for a prestigious internship? Being trapped between these bad options is another example of the double bind many women experience.

With her research in tow, Bunny outlined ways institutions could help prevent and responsibly deal with sexual harassment. Some of her many suggestions included forming advisory committees with both students and faculty, establishing clear policies covering

SEXUAL HARASSMENT: TRUE OR FALSE

page 89

the range of sexual harassment behaviors, developing a code of conduct for faculty and staff, creating specific response timeframes for institutions, and detailing who the trained first responders are so survivors will have resources and know exactly who to turn to if needed. Once established, Bunny suggested these policies and procedures be included in student handbooks and in classes on human sexuality. "Look strong," she'd remind women. "And remember that you are strong. You do have power."

Through hard work and perseverance, Bunny changed the world for future generations of women and girls. She also managed to carve a lasting place

KNOW
YOUR
TITLE IX
page 91

for herself in the women's movement and in history, right alongside the suffragists she so admired. But it wasn't always easy. Bunny stood on the frontlines of the women's movement before it was fashionable or cool to be there. Not only did she go through a divorce in 1979, but like many strong, outspoken women of the time she sometimes faced resentment and resistance for her work. While receiving the Rockefeller Public Service award in 1976, a fellow award winner told her, "You shouldn't even be here. You don't deserve that award." And while giving a speech at a peace conference at Loyola Marymount in the late 1970s, an audience member stood and heckled her, calling her the Devil and accusing her of ruining people's lives. And these are just incidents people witnessed. Most often Bunny would stoically ignore the insults, choosing the high road. She believed in taking the long view, seeing those uncomfortable moments as just bumps in the road. Of course, her bravery, steadfast determination, and a touch of Ivy's stubbornness didn't hurt either.

Bunny and daughter Emily at the Rockefeller Public Service Awards, 1976. The award recognized extraordinary public service. Bunny was the first woman outside of government to receive it.

Though Bunny worked tirelessly through her life for women's rights and equity in education, she still found ways to relax. Before her knees made it impossible, she enjoyed running. At one point, she even bought a bright orange sash to make herself more visible. It served the purpose, but really, she remembered, it was to make up for not being a crossing guard in elementary school!

Eventually, Bunny came across a book on birding. The quiet, passive activity brought her out of her many intellectual pursuits and into nature, a joy she'd found as a girl with her father, Abe. Birding also fed Bunny's introverted nature. Surprisingly, for such a strong outspoken voice in the fight for women's rights, Bunny Sandler wasn't an extrovert. And though speaking before a crowd thrilled her, she loved her time outdoors. Whether it was hiking, walks on the beach with her grandkids, or quiet time spotting birds, Bunny enjoyed a deep appreciation for nature. Over the years she took birding trips to Alaska, California, Mexico, and Costa Rica. She never tired of the peaceful spot behind her binoculars, watching the beauty and freedom she found in her beloved birds. She remained a devoted birder until her death in January 2019.

Young Bunny Sandler didn't have a word for it, but she knew it wasn't fair that only boys could fill the inkwell or run the slide projector at school. She knew girls should have the same chance as boys to be crossing guards if they wanted. She knew what injustice felt like, and she wanted to change it.

And she did. During her life Bunny was a musician and a lover of the arts. She was a devoted mother and grandmother. She became an educator, a writer, and an activist. She testified before Congress in groundbreaking hearings, and as an expert witness in many high-profile trials. She spoke frequently at colleges and universities across the world, sharing her extensive knowledge on equity in women's education, sexual harassment, and gender discrimination. She became a beloved mentor to many women and is now known as the Godmother of Title IX. Through it all she remained generous. Bunny took care to share her good fortune with friends and family over the years, and often opened her home to young people who were interning in Washington, DC.

Bunny wasn't an activist or a seasoned political operative when she discovered Executive Order 11246. She was a student and an academic—just a woman trying to get a job. But when faced with injustice, instead of shrugging it off or simply being disappointed and moving on, she put her considerable determination and skill to work. She dug in and researched, hunting and reading for months, until she found a way forward. A way paved with documented hard facts and solid psychological research that led to a future where sex discrimination in education was illegal. In Greek, Bernice means "Bringer of Victory." Bernice Resnick Sandler certainly lived up to her name.

UPPITY WOMEN UNITE

page 92

Bunny with transcripts from Edith's Green's 1970 hearings on sex discrimination in education.

And though she'd succeeded in changing the law, and the world, and much had changed since she'd been denied the chance to run that slide projector as a girl, Bunny knew the fight wasn't over. "Change is slow and often a painful process," she said in 2013. "Women's work has just begun." Still, she remained hopeful. Obstacles, no matter how big or powerful, were just bumps in the road. It was that unwavering faith in a brighter future that Bunny often chose to leave with audiences, reciting her favorite quote by Mary Chagnon:

And they shall beat their pots and pans into printing presses and weave their cloth into protest banners. Nations of women shall lift up their voices with nations of other women. Neither shall they accept discrimination anymore.

Likeability Trap

Bunny's work on Chilly Climate included the difficult position women face communicating in higher education. Because women are taught through unconscious and subtle signals to be more submissive, society often expects them to be nice, helpful, compassionate, and nurturing. Men, in contrast, are taught to be dominant. They are expected to be assertive, aggressive, and in charge.

These expectations are seen in how we talk. Commanding forms of speech like terse pronouncements, interrupting, and finger-pointing are traditionally considered "masculine." Because this style is valued in education, women face a double bind called the likeability trap.

If a woman communicates as she's been taught, she may hesitate, make a false start, or be overly polite. She may end her comment with a tag question like, "See what I mean?" or "Don't you think?" She might use qualifiers like, "sometimes" and "maybe." In addition, she's probably striving to be more collaborative. Interestingly, Bunny noted research showing women aren't the only group who speaks like this. Groups with low status or little power will often adopt similar patterns. In education, these behaviors make it likely the professor and the woman's classmates (including other women) will dismiss what she has to say as rambling, unclear, or wishy-washy. In short, unintelligent. But if she adopts the more aggressive style, she'll face a backlash for not behaving as society expects and be dismissed as abrasive or unlikeable. Clearly, she can't win. She's in the likeability trap.

And it's not a thing of the past. A 2017 study found even in the Supreme Court men interrupt more than women, and they interrupt women more than other men. We have a long way to go.

Bunny knew "feminine" communication was undervalued, placing women in the double bind, but she didn't advocate that women adopt the "masculine" style. Instead, she suggested society value "feminine" speech more, pointing to studies that examined the value of a less assertive tone and a style open to collaboration. Ideally, Bunny noted, "both men and women should be able to use both kinds of speech, depending on what is appropriate for the situation."

Sexual Harassment: True or False

You can only be sexually harassed if society thinks you're attractive.

False. Sexual harassment happens to all kinds of people, regardless of how they look. Sexual harassment is about power, as well as unwanted attention. It has nothing to do with how someone looks.

A woman's beauty can be so overpowering it causes sexual harassment.

False. Suggesting a woman's beauty could cause a man to sexually harass her does two things. First, it deflects attention from the harasser and blames the person who was harassed, which is never okay. Second, it assumes sexual harassment is an extension of a natural biological drive, instead of what it really is—an abuse of power.

The clothing you wear can cause sexual harassment.

False. People wear all kinds of clothes for all kinds of reasons. The idea that a person is "asking for it" because of what they're wearing blames the person who was harassed for the harasser's bad behavior. No matter what you're wearing, it is never an invitation for unwanted attention. As Bunny said, "Clothing does not give others permission to touch or grab."

Sexual harassment is possible between two consenting adults.

True. This sounds tricky, but it focuses on the power dynamics in a relationship. Real consent cannot happen if one person has power over the other. Think of the relationship between a boss and an employee, or a teacher and a student. One person has power over the other. Real consent isn't possible in relationships like this. It is only possible between people who are equals.

To avoid sexual harassment, it's easy to just say no at the first sign of unwanted attention.

False. People may ignore unwanted attention, or even consent to behavior they may not really want to engage in because they are afraid of the consequences if they complain or say no. When someone holds power over you, it is not always easy to say no at the first sign of unwanted attention.

Sexual harassment only happens to women.

False. Sexual harassment is an abuse of power. Because women have historically had less power in society than men, harassment against women is the most common form. But sexual harassment can happen to anyone, regardless of sex or gender.

Do you notice anything about most of these myths?

If you're thinking they put the focus (and the blame) on the person who was harassed, you're right. Such blaming is an unfortunate, and all too common, part of sexual harassment. When Bernice Sandler educated colleges and universities about sexual harassment, she made sure to address common myths.

Know Your IX

After surviving sexual assault on campus, college students Dana Bolger and Alexandra Brodsky founded Know Your IX in 2013. Through resources, activism, and outreach, the organization educates students and the public about their rights and protections under Title IX.

Notably, in 2014, through significant political pressure and grassroots lobbying, the organization forced the Department of Education to publish for the first time a list of schools across the country who were being investigated for Title IX violations related to sexual violence. The group has also been involved in a campaign leading to the Department of Education stating that schools in violation of Title IX may have to reimburse affected students for lost tuition.

Primarily an advocacy group for people who survived sexual assault, Know Your IX works nationwide to influence and change policy at all levels of government, hoping to enact meaningful change that will end gender violence in colleges and universities in the U.S.

https://www.knowyourix.org/

CHECK OUT 9 THINGS TO KNOW ABOUT TITLE IX
page 112

9 THINGS TO KNOW ABOUT TITLE IX FOR LGBTQ STUDENTS
page 114-115

DISABILITY RIGHTS & TITLE IX
page 113

Uppity Women Unite

Bunny loved to get the word out about women's rights and Title IX with political pins. She invented the UPPITY WOMEN UNITE button and always had some on hand. "I must have given out 7,000 of them," she remembered in a 2016 interview with Harvard Magazine. "The pins were an easy way to talk about women's rights because they were funny." They were also a great outlet for Bunny's spunky personality. Once, during a meeting at the Cosmos Club in Washington, DC— an exclusive club that didn't allow women to enter through the front door—Bunny put a pin on every flat surface she could find. Though staff gathered them up as fast as she put them down, Bunny got her message across. When a like-minded server discovered what she was doing, he snuck to the men's bathroom and put an UPPITY WOMEN UNITE pin on every urinal!

Left to Right. Bunny invented this UPPITY WOMEN UNITE button to raise awareness about gender equity. GOD BLESS YOU, TITLE IX, Bunny and Margaret Dunkle's first TIX button, was invented around 1974. Margaret Dunkle's love of puns inspired the iconic TIX phrase, GIVE WOMEN A "SPORTING CHANCE." She and Bunny invented this button around 1974.

The White House was fair game, too. During a dinner while she was Chair of the National Advisory Council on Women's Educational Programs, a position she held under both President Gerald Ford and President Jimmy Carter, Bunny filled her black clutch purse with nothing but buttons. Not a lipstick, a band-aid, or even her keys. By the end of the night, she'd given all the buttons away.

Around 1974, Bunny and Margaret Dunkle came up with the GOD BLESS YOU, TITLE IX button. Originals show black lettering on a yellow background. Blue versions were printed later for a speaking engagement both women gave on Title IX.

Political pins and buttons have been around for over 200 years, dating back to the fight for women's suffrage and beyond. Bunny loved political pins celebrating women and had a collection of over 1,000. Her pins are now kept at the Radcliffe Institute's Schlesinger Library in Cambridge, Massachusetts.

*Just some of the political buttons from Bunny's collection.
She had over 1,000 when she donated them to the Schlesinger
Library at Harvard University's Radcliffe Institute.*

TRY THIS:
Creative Project

Think about everything you've learned. Think about
life in the United States when Bunny was growing
up, before Title IX. Contrast that with life in the U.S.
now. What challenges do women and others still face
in the long fight for equity? Do you belong to one or
more intersecting groups that face challenges in our
society? How does it make you feel—angry, energized,
overwhelmed, or inspired and ready to fight to make
a difference?

Read through the following activities and pick
one that appeals to you. There's no wrong answer,
it's about connecting with what works for you! Use
the project to express yourself. Maybe you write a
newspaper article explaining the factual differences
between the time before Title IX and after, or maybe
you write a Letter to the Editor expressing your
feelings about gender discrimination. Maybe you
write an acrostic poem using your name, expressing
your frustration with the present or your hopes for the
future. Your project can be something you share or
keep totally private. It's completely up to you.

DIARY ENTRY: Think of a moment in Bunny's life that stood out to you. Maybe it's the moment she discovered the footnote prohibiting sex discrimination, or when she testified before Congress. Maybe it's when she first realized only boys were allowed to use the slide projector in school. Now imagine being her. How might you have felt in her situation? Write a diary entry about it from Bunny's perspective. Would you have done things differently than she did? Think about including details about how you might have thought, acted, and planned to make a difference. Or, think of a moment in your life. It might be something that's happened already, or even one you hope will happen in the future. Imagine yourself there. Write a detailed diary entry explaining how you feel in the moment and why. Consider including how you moved through the moment, or ideas on how you plan to get there.

OBITUARY: An obituary commemorates a person's accomplishments and characteristics after they've died. It usually appears in the newspaper or online. Think of someone you admire who isn't alive anymore. It could be a loved one or someone you've never met. Write an obituary for them. Be sure to note what made them special to you or how they made a difference in your life.

ACROSTIC or I AM POEM: First, think of a subject you'd like to write about, maybe a person, place, or even a social issue you're interested in. To do an acrostic poem, start by writing your subject's name vertically. Use the first letter of each line to begin a new word that describes your subject. For example, an acrostic poem of BERNICE might have BRAVE for the first line. Continue until each letter has a descriptive word.

> **Brave**
> **Energetic**
> **Resilient**
> **Notable**
> **Inspiring**
> **Charitable**
> **Enduring**

An I AM poem usually has ten lines. The first might be something like, "I am Bunny Sandler." The next nine lines will begin with I AM and continue to describe the subject. A second line in an I AM poem about Bunny might read, "I am an activist." Describe your subject with thoughtful words that express what the person or topic means to you.

COMIC STRIP: Find a funny (but influential) moment in your life or someone else's and create a comic strip that tells the story. Maybe you focus on the night Bunny put UPPITY WOMEN UNITE buttons all over a club that discriminated against women, or maybe you tell the story of the first time you went to a protest. To tell the best story here, investigate graphic arts as a genre and learn about splash panels, speech bubbles, captions, and spreads.

NEWSPAPER ARTICLE: You're a cub reporter on the job! It's up to you to get the breaking news of the day to the public. Decide on an important event in your life or someone else's and write a fact-filled news article about it. Be sure to include the essentials—who, what, when, where, why, and how.

ILLUSTRATE: Think of a situation in your life that's meaningful to you. Instead of writing about it, draw it. You might choose to draw an important moment from someone else's life that you found notable or inspiring, or from your own. Think about how shape and color are used to express emotion. Does red indicate a different emotional tone than pale grey? What does a rounded line suggest vs. a collection of hard, straight lines? Explore these things as you draw. Try to convey the same amount of information and emotion through your pictures as you would with your words.

Activities based on on Educator Guide by Deb Gonzales

How to Be an Activist

by Sage Carson

Today, so many young people are using their collective power to demand change. From youth activists fighting climate change to immigrant youth demanding a clean DREAM act, young people are building a bigger and brighter world for themselves and future generations. That's because youth organizing is powerful and has led to some of the most impactful change in our society. Take for example the Freedom Riders during the civil rights movement—the young college students who joined forces to end segregation in public spaces during the 1960s. Or the student victims of the Parkland school shooting, who sparked a national youth movement to end gun violence in schools while still trying to graduate high school.

At Know Your IX, we believe that youth organizing is so powerful because we are centering those often most impacted by the harm. As students who have faced gender discrimination and sexual harassment that impacted our ability to succeed and thrive in school, we can use our firsthand experience to inform policy change and shift our culture to create safer and more equitable schools. And we can show others who have faced the same hardships that they aren't alone—for so many, simply finding others who share your experience can be life-changing.

If you, like Bernice Sandler, want to be an activist for issues that are important to you, these tips will help you plan and implement powerful campaigns to create change.

Build your campaign.

First, identify the problems that you and people in your community are facing. For example, some schools have no resources to ensure pregnant and parenting students can still equally participate in education. This lack of support from schools has led to approximately 70% of teenage girls who give birth leaving their schools.[1] After you decide what issues you want to organize around, it's important to identify the specific ways institutions like schools, workplaces, or the government are causing harm—this will allow

---

1 Tate, D. (2008). *Schools for All Campaign: The School Bias & Pushout Problem*. ACLU of Northern California. Retrieved from: https://www.aclunc.org/sites/default/files/Schools%20 For%20All%20Campaign-%20The%20School%20Bias%20 and%20Pushout%20Problem.pdf

you to find the solution to the problems you identify. Remember, there is not a one-size-fits-all solution to fighting issues in our communities—what works at a large public school in a city might be totally different from what works at a small religious or rural school. That can make creating solutions challenging, but it also gives you the chance to shape innovative demands tailored to your community.

Next, build your team. As organizer Mariame Kaba said, "everything worthwhile is done with others." Fighting inequity is a big undertaking, and no one person can do it on their own! If you're having a hard time thinking of where to start, make a list of 10-15 people you know who you think might want to work with you. You can draw from your friends and classmates, activists you know are organizing on other issues, and the leaders and members of existing clubs or student groups. Sit down and have a one-on-one conversation with them about why this work is important and explain what you envision. Ask why they care about this issue and what motivates them. Ask if they'll get involved. From there, you'll have a group of 5-7 people who will form your core team to start the campaign.

As you're building a core team, try to reach out to people with a wide range of experiences and expertise. Your team will be stronger if your core members have a broad range of skills and interests. Even more importantly, your team will be stronger if your core group centers the people most impacted by the issue you're focusing on. When it comes to activism, one voice can't take on every issue. Make sure you're inviting other perspectives to the table, even when you're not the official organizer. Often, people's perspectives on the issue will be very different depending on their identity and experiences. For example, students who survive violence are sometimes failed by their school in different and unique ways. By working with a team that is reflective of your community, you can build solutions that will work for everyone, not just some people.

After you have your core team, work together to find concrete solutions to the issues you have identified. If you're organizing to change a school or community policy, it's important for your group to read the existing policies together to see what change needs to be made. Keep in mind that the majority of problems with your policy may be things that are not included or are not specifically articulated; your policy's biggest problems may be not with the existing content, but rather with what's missing from it. You can work as a group to make notes on the policy about what should change. Then take those notes, and make them into specific proposals. For example, instead of saying your school needs to "take sexual violence seriously," or "make our schools safer," you could require that your school hire a social worker to support students who are experiencing bullying or sexual harassment. It's much easier for your principal or mayor to say they "take something seriously" without making any change, than for them to say they support your issue while refusing to meet your specific demands.

After you've built your team and identified your issues and solutions, it's time to plan out your campaign plan. Creating a campaign strategy is essential for a strong campaign and will serve as a roadmap for your team. This road map helps us understand how we are going to "win" something before we even start organizing our first event and keeps us focused on achieving our goals.

Your strategic plan will have three essential pieces, the Three Ts: Targets, Timeline, and Tactics.

* **Target:** Who has the power to make the changes you're fighting for?

* **Timeline:** When could these decisions be made? When are your target(s) most vulnerable to pressure?

* **Tactics:** What concrete actions are you going to use to put pressure on your target(s) to make the changes you want?

Choose your target.

First, start with identifying the people in positions of power who have the ability to make the changes you are advocating for. A target is always a person, not a group, body, or institution. If you find that you are not able to work with these administrators, research other individuals or groups that could help you pressure the key power-holders. If you are trying to get prevention education in school, some of your targets might be your principal, school board members, or the health teacher.

Make a timeline to help your team stay focused!

Your timeline will outline what tactics you want to use and when. To make a timeline, it's helpful to consider these questions:

* When are decisions on this issue made? For example, a school board meeting or during a legislative session.

* When are decision-makers vulnerable? Parent's night, sports games, assemblies, or during public speeches are good examples of times when decision-makers might be more vulnerable to pressure.

* When can you get the most publicity? The summer or winter vacations are tough times to get media attention.

* When is your team the strongest? Times where big tests or events are happening might not be a good time for your team to plan big events.

Decide what tactics you want to use.

Tactics are the actions, events, and activities that make up your campaign. They will often vary depending on the target: a tactic that works to influence a teacher will look very different from one that works to pressure the head of your school board. Flexible, resourceful, and creative tactics are great for attracting attention to your campaign and keeping your strategy fresh. For example, after former Secretary of Education Betsy DeVos refused to meet with student survivors about Title IX, we launched the campaign "#DearBetsy." The hashtag allowed survivors to share their stories and experiences with the secretary and sparked a national conversation about the needs of student survivors in school. The tactics you select at various points during your campaign could be influenced by your campaign's size, energy, and resources, the strengths and styles of your current activists, the specific targets you're trying to influence, and other factors.

Tactics typically fall into one of three categories:

Base-Building tactics help you build your list of supporters and bring new members on board with your campaign. Examples include tabling at student activity fairs or sports games, making a petition and collecting signatures, or pitching lunch tables about your campaign and asking them to join.

Educational tactics help educate your base about the campaign, the issues, and your goals. These might include teach-ins, poster campaigns, trainings, speak outs, sharing stories, and articles or op-eds.

Power tactics are the actions your organization and allies undertake to pressure your targets to meet your demands. Protests, event interruptions, and petition deliveries are good examples of power tactics. A power tactic typically is never the first time your target is learning about your demands; for example, you don't want to plan a huge protest blasting your target, the vice-principal, for not meeting your demands if it's the first time they are learning about your demands. Power tactics are what you do to win, but educational and base-building tactics are crucial to building awareness and community support. Other examples of tactics include press conferences, media events, public hearings or forums, strikes, and creative and performance pieces.

Sharing your story is a great way to be an activist for the issues that matter to you. For some, deciding whether to go public with your story is an easy and obvious yes. For others, it's a tough call and one that changes over the course of a few weeks, months, or years. For all of us, it's a decision only we can each make for ourselves. At the end of the day, this is your experience, your activism, your life, and your decision.

For many, the issues we choose to organize around are personal. Because of that, our personal stories can serve as powerful mechanisms for change and help build a better world. Stories can help people better understand the issue, provide people with hope, and make us feel more connected to others. Our stories can also humanize the issue—taking statistics and facts and turning them into human faces who are affected by the policies and inequalities.

If you're considering sharing stories to support your activism, here are some questions to consider to help you create your "story of self."

1. What am I asking others to do?

2. What is important to me and inspired me to take action? Could those same things inspire others to take action?

3. What stories can I tell from my own life that would show (rather than tell) why this action or change is important to me?

Then, think about the challenge, choice, and outcome in your story—the challenges you faced, the choices you made, and the outcomes you experienced.

* **Challenge:** Why was it a challenge? What was so challenging about it?

* **Choice:** Why did you make the choices you did? What brought you the courage to make that choice? Or why were you forced to make the choice you did?

* **Outcome:** How did the outcome feel? What lessons did you learn? What do you want to teach us? How do you want us to feel?

By sharing meaningful stories, we can make a big difference! Whether you're giving a speech, posting on social media, or talking to your peers, your story can spur someone to take action or make someone with a similar story feel less alone.

Whether you're launching a campaign in your school, telling your story to spur community change, or creating posters about an issue important to you, there is no one way to be an activist. You don't have to be the loudest person in the room to make a difference, you just have to do your best to build towards a brighter and better future. Who knows, maybe one day you'll be changing the world, just like Bernice Sandler.

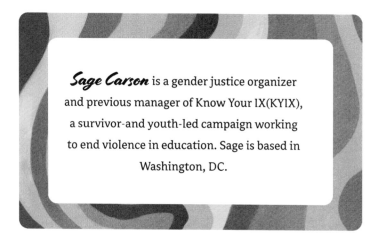

Sage Carson is a gender justice organizer and previous manager of Know Your IX(KYIX), a survivor-and youth-led campaign working to end violence in education. Sage is based in Washington, DC.

9 THINGS TO KNOW
ABOUT TITLE IX

1 Title IX is a civil right that prohibits sex discrimination in education.

2 Title IX applies to all students regardless of gender identity.

3 All schools receiving federal funding, including public K-12 schools and the majority of colleges, are subject to Title IX.

4 Schools cannot discourage you from continuing your education.

5 Schools can issue no-contact directives to prevent accused students from approaching or interacting with you.

6 Schools must have an established procedure for handling complaints of sexual discrimination, harassment, and violence.

7 Schools should ensure that no student has to share campus spaces (such as dorms, classes, and workplaces) with their abuser.

8 Schools may not retaliate against someone filing a complaint and must keep complaints safe from other retaliatory harassment.

9 Schools must be proactive in ensuring that your campus is free from sex discrimination.

LEARN MORE AT
KNOWYOURIX.ORG

KNOW YOUR IX
A PROJECT OF ADVOCATES FOR YOUTH

DISABILITY RIGHTS AND TITLE IX

1 Title IX is a civil rights law that prohibits sex discrimination in all levels of education— and does not require schools to take any actions inconsistent with laws that protect students with disabilities.

2 Title IX applies to all students, including students with disabilities.

3 Your school must provide you with disability accommodations to ensure that a disability doesn't prevent you from staying in school, and that you have access to therapy, classroom changes, extensions on school assignments, no–contact orders, and other reasonable accommodations.

4 Your right to reasonable disability accommodations under Section 504 and/or the ADA includes accommodations for both prior disabilities and disabilities caused by harassment or violence.

5 Your school cannot refuse you services offered to people without disabilities, such as accessible emergency housing.

6 Your school buildings and offices related to an investigation must be accessible, including the Title IX offices, disability offices, counseling centers, emergency housing, and medical centers.

7 Your school must conclude your investigation in a timely manner and cannot unreasonably delay your investigation because of a request for a reasonable disability accommodation.

8 Schools should allow you to answer questions in writing or through a neutral school employee if your disability makes it difficult to answer questions in a live cross–examination format.

9 You have the right to have physical, mental, and emotional disabilities treated equally.

LEARN MORE AT KNOWYOURIX.ORG

KNOW YOUR IX

A PROJECT OF ADVOCATES FOR YOUTH

9 THINGS TO KNOW ABOUT TITLE IX

FOR LGBTQ+ STUDENTS

1 Title IX is a civil rights law that prohibits sex discrimination in education.

2 Transgender students are protected by Title IX, which ensures they have the right to equal access to educational opportunities, including access to single-sex spaces and activities consistent with their gender identity.

3 Title IX protects all students who experience sexual violence and gender discrimination, regardless of the gender of the survivor or the named perpetrator(s).

6 Schools' obligations to appropriately respond to sexual violence and support a survivor's continued access to education are the same regardless of the sexual orientation, gender identity, and/or gender presentation of a complainant or respondent; this remains true when incidents of sexual violence may be partly based on a survivor's (actual or perceived) sexual orientation or gender identity.

7 Schools must investigate and remedy instances of sexual violence against LGBTQ+ students using the same policies and procedures used in all complaints of sexual violence.

Infographics provided by KNOW YOUR IX. Reprinted with permission.

4 LGBTQ+ survivors of sexual violence or victims of discrimination have the same rights under Title IX to accommodations, a prompt and equitable complaint process, and freedom from retaliation.

5 Title IX requires schools to respect transgender students' gender identity with regard to dress codes, names, pronouns, and access to single-sex facilities (including restrooms). Facilities should be accessible to all who require them and not prohibited by age.

8 Title IX protects transgender and gender nonconforming students from gender-based harassment and bullying — that is, harassment or bullying a student experiences because they do not conform to stereotypical notions of masculinity and femininity.

9 Transgender students should have access to reasonable accommodations that respect their gender identity, such as gender inclusive emergency housing.

If your school isn't respecting your rights, you have options.
Learn more and get involved at www.knowyourIX.org

More Photos From Bernice's Life

Bunny, February 1947.

Bunny in the late 1950s.

Bunny in the early 1950s.

Project on the Status & Education of Women staff, 1977.

Bunny's smile was infectious.

Bunny's favorite binoculars for birdwatching, and other gear.

Bunny, the day she was inducted into the National Women's Hall of Fame, 2013.

Margaret Dunkle and Bunny at Bunny's 90th birthday party, held at the Woman's National Democratic Club in Washington, DC, 2018.

Photo Credits

Introduction

Margaret Dunkle, age 8, playing badminton in her front yard, 1955. Photo courtesy of Margaret Dunkle. Reprinted with permission.

Margaret Dunkle and Bunny, 1977. Photo courtesy of Margaret Dunkle. Reprinted with permission.

Chapter 2

Bunny (right) with her big sister Rhoda, 1934. Photo courtesy of Emily Sandler. Reprinted with permission.

Cooking class, Bethesda-Chevy Chase High School, 1935. From Library of Congress, National Photo Company Collection [LC-F8112- 44610 P&P].

Bunny's daughters Emily and Deborah, with Ivy, at Resnick's, 1962. From the Sandler family collection, courtesy of the National Women's Hall of Fame Oral History Project, Institute of Museum and Library Services. Reprinted with permission.

Bunny and Jerry Sandler, 1952. Photo courtesy of Emily Sandler. Reprinted with permission.

Bunny and her daughter Emily, 1958. Courtesy of Emily Sandler. Reprinted with permission.

Chapter 3

Bunny's WEAL membership card for 1975. Photo courtesy of Schlesinger Library, Harvard Radcliffe Institute.

"First Dollar" by cartoonist Doug Marlette, 1982. Copyright by Melinda Marlette. Reprinted with permission.

Vince Macaluso and Bernice Sandler, 2009. Photo courtesy of Veteran Feminists of America. Reprinted with permission.

Bunny at work, 1971. Photo courtesy of Emily Sandler. Reprinted with permission.

Bunny was passionate about the fight for Washington, DC statehood and proudly displayed this license plate. Copyright by Emily Sandler. Reprinted with permission.

Chapter 4

Male Only/Female Only Want Ads in The Washington Times, 1915. From Library of Congress. Chronicling America: Historic American Newspapers.

Poster created by Albert M. Bender for the WPA between 1936 and 1941. From the Library of Congress, Prints & Photographs Division, WPA Collection [LC-USZ62-117504].

Bunny (center) and colleagues with Senator Birch Bayh (right). From the Sandler family collection, courtesy of the National Women's Hall of Fame Oral History Project, Institute of Museum and Library Services. Reprinted with permission.

Chapter 5

Bunny (far left) in a meeting with Walter Mondale (far right), the 42nd Vice President. From the Sandler family collection, courtesy of the National Women's Hall of Fame Oral History Project, Institute of Museum and Library Services. Reprinted with permission.

Chris Ernst in Director of Physical Education Joni Barnett's office at Yale, protesting gender inequity. Photo by Nina Haight, March 3, 1976. Copyright Yale Daily News Publishing Co., Inc. All rights reserved. Reprinted with permission.

Students protesting their school's mishandling of sexual violence at graduation. Photo courtesy of Know Your IX. Reprinted with permission.

Chapter 6

Bunny and daughter Emily at the Rockefeller Public Service Awards, 1976. From the Sandler family collection, courtesy of the National Women's Hall of Fame Oral History Project, Institute of Museum and Library Services. Reprinted with permission.

Bunny with transcripts from Edith's Green's 1970 hearings on sex discrimination in education. From the Sandler family collection, courtesy of the National Women's Hall of Fame Oral History Project, Institute of Museum and Library Services. Reprinted with permission.

Title IX buttons, 1974. Photo courtesy of Schlesinger Library, Harvard Radcliffe Institute. Reprinted with permission.

Political Buttons. Photo by Jim Harrison, courtesy of Schlesinger Library, Harvard Radcliffe Institute. Reprinted with permission.

More Photos From Bernice's Life

Bunny, February 1947. Photo courtesy of Emily Sandler. Reprinted with permission.

Bunny in the early 1950s. Photo courtesy of Emily Sandler. Reprinted with permission.

Bunny in the late 1950s. Photo courtesy of Emily Sandler. Reprinted with permission.

Project on the Status & Education of Women staff, 1977. Copyright by Margaret Dunkle. Courtesy of Margaret Dunkle's personal collection. Reprinted with permission.

Bunny's smile was infectious. Copyright by Deborah Jo Sandler. Courtesy of the Sandler family collection. Reprinted with permission.

Bunny's favorite binoculars for birdwatching, and other gear. Copyright by Deborah Jo Sandler. Courtesy of the Sandler family collection. Reprinted with permission.

Bunny, the day she was inducted into the National Women's Hall of Fame, 2013. Copyright by Deborah Jo Sandler. Courtesy of the Sandler family collection. Reprinted with permission.

Margaret Dunkle and Bunny at Bunny's 90th birthday party, held at the Woman's National Democratic Club in Washington, DC, 2018. Photo by Carol McCabe Booker. Courtesy of Margaret Dunkle. Reprinted with permission.

 # Bibliography

A American Psychological Association. (2012). APA Presidential
       Citation awarded to Dr. Bernice "Bunny" Sandler. Retrieved
       from: https://www.apa.org/pi/women/resources/news/
       citation-sandler

B Bayer, B. M. (2016, September 16). *Interview with Bernice R.
       Sandler*. National Women's Hall of Fame. Retrieved from:
       https://www.womenofthehall.org/women-of-the-hall/voices-
       great-women/bernice-resnick-sandler/

   Bolotnikova, M. N. (2016, November-December). Pins for Women:
       A Century of Mini Political Mileposts. *Harvard Magazine*.
       Retrieved from: https://www.harvardmagazine.com/2016/11/
       pins-for-women

   Blumenthal, K. (2005). *Let Me Play: The Story of Title IX, the Law
       That Changed the Future of Girls in America*. Atheneum.

   Boschert, S. (2015, January 29). Name It to Change It. Retrieved
       from http://www.sherryboschert.com/name-it-change-it-
       bernice-sandler/

   Boschert, S. (2015, February 15). Fresno Tied to Title IX Over
       Decades. Retrieved from http://www.sherryboschert.com/
       fresno-tied-title-ix-decades/

   Boschert, S. (2015, February 21). The Uppity Women Behind Title
       IX. Retrieved from http://www.sherryboschert.com/page/2/

Boschert, S. (2015, June 18). Spotting Truthiness in Title IX Debates. Retrieved from http://www.sherryboschert.com/spotting-truthiness-title-ix-debates/

Boschert, S. (2015, July 21). Legal Muscle Behind Title IX Still Flexing. Retrieved from: http://www.sherryboschert.com/page/2/

Boschert, S. (2015, September 14). My Title IX Reading List (Or What I Did This Summer). Retrieved from: http://www.sherryboschert.com/my-title-ix-reading-list-what-i-did-this-summer/

Boschert, S. (2016, November 28). Title IX Advocates Say Black Lives Matter. Retrieved from: http://www.sherryboschert.com/title-ix-advocates-say-black-lives-matter/

Bridgeman, J. (2019). Profile of Bernice Resnick Sandler. In A. Rutherford (Ed.), *Psychology's Feminist Voices Multimedia Internet Archive*. Retrieved from https://feministvoices.com/profiles/bernice-resnick-sandler

Brooke-Marciniak, B. A., & de Verona, D. (2016, August 25). *Amazing Things Happen When You Give Female Athletes the Same Funding as Men*. World Economic Forum. Retrieved from: https://www.weforum.org/agenda/2016/08/sustaining-the-olympic-legacy-women-sports-and-public-policy/

Center for Inquiry. (2013, January 23). *Bernice Sandler: "The Chilly Climate: How Women Are Often Treated Differently in Subtle Unnoticed Ways by Men and Women Alike."* [Video]. YouTube. Retrieved from: https://www.youtube.com/watch?v=kyT3uW9lb9E

Chaffee, I. (2017, September 12). *Forget About Sexism: Now TV Coverage of Women's Sports is Just Plain Boring*. USC News. Retrieved from: https://news.usc.edu/127695/forget-about-sexism-now-tv-coverage-of-womens-sports-is-just-plain-boring/

Clymer, A. (2019, March 4). Birch Bayh, 91, Dies; Senator Drove Title IX and 2 Amendments. *The New York Times*. Retrieved from: https://www.nytimes.com/2019/03/14/obituaries/birch-bayh-dead.html

D   Department of Education. (2021, August). *Title IX and Sex Discrimination*. Retrieved from: https://www2.ed.gov/print/about/offices/list/ocr/docs/tix_dis.html

Donegan, A. (2017). Women in the 1930s and 1940s. *History 18.2: U.S. Women's History from 1877*. Santa Rosa Junior College.

E   Esther Eggertsen Peterson. (n.d.). AFL-CIO. Retrieved from https://aflcio.org/about/history/labor-history-people/esther-peterson

F   FingerLakesOne.com, Inc. (2013, October 21). *National Women's Hall of Fame 24th Induction Ceremony*. [Video]. YouTube. Retrieved from: https://www.youtube.com/watch?v=R7Sf6Zt7ExM

G   Gates, M. F. [@melindagates]. (2019, January 9). Dr. Bernice Sandler leaves behind an extraordinary legacy. She spent decades fighting for our rights to learn, to [Thumbnail with link attached] [Tweet]. Twitter. https://twitter.com/melindagates/status/1083035670820483072.

Gilder, G. (2017, July 12). *Millennials Can't Even Protest Right*. The Daily Beast. Retrieved from: https://www.thedailybeast.com/millennials-cant-even-protest-right

Gonzales, D. (n.d.). *The Educator's Guide*. Guides by Deb. Retrieved from: https://guidesbydeb.com/

Hall, R. M., & Sandler, B. R. (1982). *The Classroom Climate: A Chilly One for Women?* Association of American Colleges. and Universities. Retrieved from https://www.aacu.org/sites/default/files/files/publications/Classroom_Climate_ChilyOne.pdf

Harrison, C. (1988). *On Account of Sex: The Politics of Women's Issues, 1945-1968*. University of California Press. http://ark.cdlib.org/ark:/13030/ft367nb2ts/

Hirschfield Davis, J. & Apuzzo, M. (2016, May 12). U.S. Directs Public Schools to Allow Transgender Access to Restrooms. *The New York Times*. Retrieved from https://nyti.ms/3DLnosl

History of Women in Sports. (n.d.). Elmira College. Retrieved from: http://faculty.elmira.edu/dmaluso/sports/timeline/gymnastics.html

How to Conduct a Journalistic Interview. (n.d.). Scholastic. Retrieved from https://www.scholastic.com/teachers/articles/teaching-content/how-conduct-journalistic-interview/

International Olympic Committee. *When Did Women First Compete in the Olympic Games?* (n.d.). Retrieved from: https://olympics.com/ioc/faq/history-and-origin-of-the-games/when-did-women-first-compete-in-the-olympic-games

International Olympic Committee. (2020, May 28). *Female Membership of IOC Commissions Reaches an All-Time High of 47.7 per cent-Two New Female Chairs*. Retrieved from: https://olympics.com/ioc/news/female-membership-of-ioc-commissions-reaches-an-all-time-high-of-47-7-per-cent-two-new-female-chairs

 Jhangiani, R. (n.d.). *Research Methods in Social Psychology*. NOBA. Retrieved from https://nobaproject.com/modules/research-methods-in-social-psychology

 Katschwar, B. (2014, March). *Women, Sports, and Development: Does it Pay to Let Girls Play?* Peterson Institute for International Economics. Retrieved from: https://www.piie.com/publications/pb/pb14-8.pdf

Kiernan, D. (2001, February/March). The Little Law That Could. *Ms. Magazine*. 18-25.

Know Your IX. (n.d.). https://www.knowyourix.org

 Lange, D. (2020). *Share of Female Participants in the Olympic Summer Games* from 1900 to 2016. Statista. Retrieved from: https://www.statista.com/statistics/531146/women-participants-in-olympic-summer-games/

Lange, D. (2020). *Share of Accredited Coaches at the Olympic Games from 2010 to 2016, by Gender*. Statista. Retrieved from: https://www.statista.com/statistics/1118567/olympic-coaches-gender/

Lee, J., & Dusenbery, M. *Charts: The State of Women's Athletics, 40 Years After Title IX*. (2012, June 22). *Mother Jones*. Retrieved from:

https://www.motherjones.com/politics/2012/06/charts-womens-athletics-title-nine-ncaa/

LePage, B. *What's Next for Title IX?* Future Ed. September 8, 2021. Retrieved from https://www.future-ed.org/whats-next-for-title-ix/

 McLaughlin, K. (2014, August 25). *5 Things Women Couldn't Do in the Sixties.* CNN. Retrieved from: https://www.cnn.com/2014/08/07/living/sixties-women-5-things/index.html

Miss America: A History. (n.d.). Retrieved from: https://www.missamerica.org/organization/history/

MoCoCouncilMD. (2012, November 8). *MC Human Rights Hall of Fame – Dr. Bernice Sandler interview.* [Video]. YouTube. Retrieved from: https://www.youtube.com/watch?v=L3rcq4XCAM0

Morrison, P. (Host). (2017, August 15). *Women's rights campaigner Bernice Sandler: Evaluates the 37-word law that helped women to make the big plays in sports and in the classroom.* [Audio podcast episode]. In *Pat Morrison Asks.* Simplecast. Retrieved from: https://podcasts.apple.com/us/podcast/womens-rights-campaigner-bernice-sandler-evaluates/id1074119510?i=1000391058650

 National Women's Hall of Fame. (2019, January 11). *Hall Mourns Bernice "Bunny" Sandler.* Retrieved from: https://www.womenofthehall.org/hall-mourns-bernice-bunny-sandler/

National Women's Law Center & Poverty & Race Research Action Council. (n.d.). *Finishing Last: Girls of Color and School Sports*

Opportunities. Retrieved from: https://nwlc.org/wp-content/ uploads/2015/08/final_nwlc_girlsfinishinglast_report.pdf

National Women's Law Center. (n.d.). *History*. Retrieved from https://nwlc.org/about/history/.

Pennepacker, P. (2021, April 27). *The Title IX Coordinator: Roles and Responsibilities*. National Federation of State High School Associations. Retrieved from https://www.nfhs.org/articles/ the-title-ix-coordinator-roles-and-responsibilities/

Peterson, E. (1970, February 11.) *Esther E. Peterson, Oral History Interview—JFK#3, 2/11/1970*. [Transcript]. John F. Kennedy Library. Retrieved from https://www.jfklibrary.org/ sites/default/files/archives/JFKOH/Peterson%2C%20 Esther%20E/JFKOH-EEP-04/JFKOH-EEP-04-TR.pdf

President's Commission on the Status of Women. (n.d.). Encyclopedia Britannica. Retrieved from: https://www. britannica.com/topic/Presidents-Commission-on-the-Status- of-Women

Rogers, K. (2021, June 17).Title IX Protections Extend to Transgender Students, Education Dept. Says. *The New York Times*. Retrieved from https://www.nytimes. com/2021/06/16/us/politics/title-ix-transgender-students. html

Sandler, B. (1976). Presentation IV. *Signs, 1*(3), 273-277. Retrieved from http://www.jstor.org.hollins.idm.oclc.org/ stable/3173014

Sandler, B. (1987). Comparisons Missing. *Change, 19*(6), 6-6.
Retrieved from http://www.jstor.org.hollins.idm.oclc.org/
stable/40177630

Sandler, B. R. (1990). Sexual Harassment: A New Issue for
Institutions. *Initiatives, 54*, 5-10.

Sandler, B. R. (2007). Title IX: How We Got It and What a
Difference It Made. *Cleveland State Law Review, 55* (4).
Retrieved from: https://engagedscholarship.csuohio.edu/
clevstlrev/vol55/iss4/4

Sandler, B. R. (1991). Women Faculty at Work in the
Classroom, or, Why It Still Hurts to Be a Woman in
Labor. *Communication Education, 40* (1), 6-15.

Sandler, D. (2019, September 17). Personal interview with
J. Barton.

Sandler, B., Dunkle, M. C., Gleaves, F., Meckes-Jones, K., &
Shapiro, B. A (1974). *What Constitutes Equality for Women in
Sport?:* Association of American Colleges. Retrieved from
https://msa.maryland.gov/megafile/msa/speccol/sc3500/
sc3520/015800/015858/pdf/sports_report.pdf

Seelye, K. Q. (2019, January 8). Bernice Sandler, 'Godmother
of Title IX', Dies at 90. *The New York Times*. Retrieved from
https://www.nytimes.com/2019/01/08/obituaries/
bernice-sandler-dead.html

Simonson, J. (n.d.). *The Rise and Decline of the Advisory Council
on Women's Educational Equity*. Retrieved from https://www.
napequity.org/nape-content/uploads/NACWEP.pdf

Smith, B. (2019, March 14). *Former Indiana Sen. Birch Bayh—"A Great Hoosier."* NPR. Retrieved from: https://www.npr.org/2019/03/14/703578607/former-indiana-sen-birch-bayh-a-great-hoosier

Smith, T. (2014, August 12). *How Campus Sexual Assaults Came to Command New Attention.* NPR. Retrieved from: https://www.npr.org/2014/08/12/339822696/how-campus-sexual-assaults-came-to-command-new-attention

Steenbergen, C. (n.d.). *Women's Equity Action League.* Encyclopedia Britannica. Retrieved from: https://www.britannica.com/topic/Womens-Equity-Action-League

University of St. Francis. (2016). *Spotlight Interview Featuring the Godmother of Title IX, Bernice Sandler.* [Video]. Retrieved from: https://vimeo.com/159738719

U. S. Congress, Committee on Education and Labor. (1970). *Discrimination Against Women, Part 1.* [Record of congressional hearings]. Pennsylvania State University. Retrieved from: https://hdl.handle.net/2027/pst.000033116709

U. S. Congress, Committee on Education and Labor. (1970). *Discrimination Against Women, Part 2.* [Record of congressional hearings]. Pennsylvania State University. Retrieved from: https://hdl.handle.net/2027/pst.000033116716

U.S. Department of Education. (2011). *Dear Colleague Letter: Sexual Violence.* Retrieved from https://www2.ed.gov/about/offices/list/ocr/letters/colleague-201104.pdf

U.S. Department of Justice, U.S. Department of Education. (2016). *Dear Colleague Letter on Transgender Students*. Retrieved from https://www2.ed.gov/about/offices/list/ocr/letters/colleague-201605-title-ix-transgender.pdf

U.S. House of Representatives: History, Art & Archives. (n.d.). *Green, Edith Starrett*. Retrieved from: https://history.house.gov/People/Detail/14080

U.S. House of Representatives: History, Art & Archives. (n.d.). *Mink, Patsy Takemoto*. Retrieved from: https://history.house.gov/People/Detail/18329#biography

Veteran Feminists of America, Inc. (n.d.). *2009 archives*. Retrieved from: https://www.veteranfeministsofamerica.org/legacy/VFA2009%20BackPages.htm

Wambach, A. [@AbbyWambach]. (2019, January 9). Thank you Bernice Sandler!! You gave me my chance at a great life and your impact will forever be felt by [Thumbnail with link attached] [Tweet]. Twitter. https://twitter.com/AbbyWambach/status/1083215339394080768.

What Is Title IX? (n.d.). The Myra Sadker Foundation. Retrieved from: https://www.sadker.org/TitleIX.html

Wilson, S. (1998, February 2). IOC Says All New Sports Must Include Women. *The Washington Post*. Retrieved from: https://www.washingtonpost.com/wp-srv/sports/longterm/olympics1998/sport/articles/ioc2.htm

About the Author

Jen Barton is the author of six books for kids, including *What's Your Story, Amelia Earhart?* (Lerner Classroom), *What's Your Story, Harriet Tubman?* (Lerner Classroom), and *School Shootings* (BrightPoint Press). Jen lives in Pennsylvania.

Visit jbartonbooks.com.

About the Illustrator

Sarah Green is an illustrator and designer from San Francisco and a graduate of Rhode Island School of Design. Sarah lives in San Francisco, California, and Vancouver, Canada.

Visit sarahgreenillustration.com, @s_green_bean on Twitter, and @sarahgreenstudio on Instagram.

About Magination Press

Magination Press is the children's book imprint of the American Psychological Association.

Visit maginationpress.org and @MaginationPress on Facebook, Twitter, Instagram, and Pinterest.